FUNNY YOU SHOULD ASK HOW TO MAKE A WEBSITE

THE 100% NOT-BORING GUIDE TO SETTING UP YOUR WEBSITE WITH WORDPRESS

LORI CULWELL

Copyright © 2021 by LORI CULWELL

All rights reserved.

No part of this book may be reproduced in any form or by any electronic or mechanical means, including information storage and retrieval systems, without written permission from the author, except for the use of brief quotations in a book review.

Noncommercial — You may not use this work for commercial purposes.

No Derivative Works — You may not alter, transform, or build upon this work.

LEGAL NOTICE

The Publisher has strived to be as accurate and complete as possible in the creation of this report, notwithstanding the fact that they do not warrant or represent at any time that the contents within are accurate due to the rapidly changing nature of the Internet.

While all attempts have been made to verify information provided in this publication, the Publisher assumes no responsibility for errors, omissions, or contrary interpretation of the subject matter herein. Any perceived slights of specific persons, peoples, or organizations are unintentional.

In practical advice books, like anything else in life, there are no guarantees of income made. Readers are cautioned to rely on their own judgment about their individual circumstances to act accordingly.

The electronic version of this book contains affiliate links, meaning the publisher earns a small (very, very small) commission if purchases are made.

GET FREE UPDATES!

Before we get started, I want to get you set up with a way to get future updates for this book. The world of websites is dynamic and constantly evolving. As such, I make frequent updates to this guide and re-publish it at least once a quarter so all of the information is the most current it can be.

Why am I telling you this?

Here's the thing– *I* want to provide you with the most updated version of this book (whenever there is a new one) and am happy to give it to you for free, but once you buy it, I have no way to send you the update. Contrary to popular belief, Amazon (or whatever other platform you bought this book on) is not going to automatically push out the most updated version of the book to people who have already bought it. That kind of sucks, and I'm trying to change that, one book at a time.

So, here's my request: please go over here and sign up for updates. Whenever I put out a new version of this book, I will immediately notify you that it's time to download your updated copy of the eBook version. To further incentivize you, I will also give you a free copy of the companion guide I created for this book!

If you bought the eBook version originally, great! You'll simply download the updated version and move on.

If you bought the paperback, also great!! You'll get a free eBook version with free updates to go along with it

So, come on over to https://loriculwell.com/htmaw. There is a ton of information coming out about websites and Wordpress all the time, and I don't want you to miss out!

CONTENTS

1. What's Going on Here? Where Am I? and Other Questions ... 1
2. Get Yourself Organized! ... 13
3. Keyword Research! Fun! ... 17
4. The "Who What and Why" of Your Site ... 23
5. All About Domains ... 35
6. Get Some Hosting! ... 59
7. Connect Domain with Hosting ... 79
8. Install WordPress ... 87
9. The Basic Setup ... 97
10. How Will it Look? ... 109
11. Free Themes ... 113
12. Paid Themes/ Theme Builders ... 119
13. Fine! Hire a Designer! ... 129
14. Add Content & Plugins ... 137
15. The Big Reveal! ... 151
16. Now What?! ... 163
17. Bonus Material (Domains) ... 173
18. You Made It!! ... 185

What Else Can I Teach You? ... 187

1

WHAT'S GOING ON HERE? WHERE AM I? AND OTHER QUESTIONS

Hi there! Welcome! You're reading this because a) you want to try to make a website, b) you read something else I wrote and you find me mildly amusing (plus you want to make a website), or c) you're lost.

Whatever the reason, I'm glad you're here!

In this guide, I'm going to walk you through how to build a website from beginning to end, using a software called WordPress as the framework and structure. And while I'm going to be very thorough, I will try to present all of it in a way that's a little more palatable than your standard, boring website setup guide.

Like, if you called me for advice about website stuff, sure, I'd break down all the tech for you. But I'd also make you laugh along the way (or, you know, I would try). This approach will come in handy, because I'm not going to lie to you, people. Some of the technical stuff is pretty hairy, and you're going to want to quit. That's where the laughter comes in, which will hopefully help you hang in there. And you're going to want to, because listen: Learning all of this stuff is going to save you *so much money.*

Seriously. Just so, so much money. It'll also save you time. Way too often, people waste large amounts of money on parts of the setup process that only need to be done once. My guide will not only keep you from doing that, but it'll also empower you to launch that website you've been contemplating!

Together, we will go through the setup process step by step, and I'll tell you along the way what you absolutely need, what you should probably have, and what you can confidently say no to. What you'll end up with is a solid, functional website that *you* control, all at a very reasonable cost.

While we're on the subject of money, I really do want to dispel the notion that you need to lay out a bunch of cash to have a good website. This guide is for the small businessperson, author, entrepreneur, or basically anyone who simply needs a solid website to start building an audience, and who doesn't have a ton of extra money to do it. My bare-bones approach is not fancy, but it is effective, and it has been tried and tested by actual people! Plus, when you build your website yourself and use it to grow your business, you can then take that extra money and re-invest it into making your site and your business even better (something I call "bootstrapping"). What could be more empowering than that?

. . .

To get things off on the right foot, I will now attempt to read your mind and guess some of the things you may be wondering about. The first question is probably something like:

Who are you? Why should I listen to you?

Good question! Why should you follow my guidance on this particular topic?

Several reasons. Not only have I spent the majority of my career working on websites for large corporations (as a content strategist/SEO expert), but I have also worked on and built many, many sites for smaller businesses, authors, artists, doctors, and everyone in between.

In 2009, I wrote a book called "Million Dollar Website," the purpose of which was to boil down all of the insights I had acquired over years of working at big agencies and for big companies so that small businesses (and other regular people with websites) could take those insights and use them to make big improvements. After it was published, I consistently heard from readers about how much the guide helped them make changes to their websites that drove more business their way.

That book did well and people liked it, but I still felt like something was missing. I always wanted people to be able to build and update their own websites. So when WordPress eventually came around, I was thrilled because finally, here was software that actually puts web development into the hands of regular people.

However, because my other website book came out through a traditional publisher, there was no time to go back and include a section on making your site from scratch out of WordPress. That's why I started this guide as a supplement, and have been adding to it (and sending it to people as an instructional guide) ever since. I recently noticed this guide had grown to be almost 200 pages long, so, with some of my "free time" during the pandemic, I decided to finally pull it together and publish it!

Who is this guide for?

Some of the people I think will benefit from this guide are:

1. Total beginners who just have zero idea how to start. This guide will take you through every step of the setup process, with the finished result being a website that you set up and that you control. Both of these things will be super helpful if and when you decide to hire someone to spruce up your website because you'll understand the process, and you won't be at risk of letting someone else have control of your site (I'll explain what I mean here later).

2. Anyone with a website on a "free" platform like Blogger, Wix, or wordpress.com. These sites aren't really free, of course, and they lack functionality, something that can really hold you back. In this guide, you'll learn why you're *so* much better off with a site you own and manage.

3. Anyone who already has a website and who just wants to take more control over management and maintenance—or who wants to learn more and empower themselves in order to save money. I'm here for that!

What am I really going to learn here?

Ideally, by the end of this guide, you will be able to:

• Get yourself so organized, you never waste time looking for a username or password ever again.

• Do basic keyword research to gauge the demand for your concept and get ideas for content right off the bat.

• Confidently buy and register a domain for about $12.

• Negotiate for a premium domain, if you have your heart set on that.

• Select and sign up for hosting without spending a zillion dollars or getting lost in upsells.

• Install WordPress as the "architecture" of your website.

• Get your website looking the way you want, either by using a free or paid theme or by hiring someone to design it for you.

• Pick and install plugins that make your website do what you want it to do.

• Learn what settings to change at the very beginning to save yourself hours (days, even!) of time and hassle.

• Learn about and get started on an actual million-dollar content strategy that I have been using and testing for over 20 years (this is pretty much worth the price of admission all by itself, people).

• Set your website up to do automatic maintenance, but still be able to calmly troubleshoot it if it crashes.

Okay, that might have sounded like a little much, but you can do it. I believe in you! I know this sounds ambitious, but it'll be worth it. My honest goal is to ensure that by the time you are done reading this book, you will never be at a disadvantage in a tech conversation again. Never again will someone charge you money because they know more about tech stuff than you!

We are going to take all of this step by step and keep it super simple, with lots of explanations along the way so you don't get lost. Plus, it's just us here, so no one will know if you have to read a section ten times or swear a lot to get through it. No pressure!

How difficult is this going to be?

. . .

I've said this already, but it bears repeating: The first time you go through this guide, you're going to want to quit (or at least send me some mean emails), especially when you get to the part about setting up the hosting, installing WordPress, and tweaking the settings until your website does exactly what you want it to do. The first time through, you might want to throw up your hands and turn your website back over to someone else to build and manage. Don't do it! Building and maintaining your website is a skill that will save you hundreds (if not thousands) of dollars, and it's one you can use again and again! It gets easier every time you do it!

Why WordPress? Why not a full-on html site (or Wix, or Squarespace)?

It's not that I don't like those types of websites. Some of them look great! Here's a brief run-down on why I don't use them, in order of my personal irritation level:

1. Html sites are looking more and more old-school each year, plus they're really hard to update. You're not going to want to update your blog if you have to crack open your site and write a bunch of code to do it. Trust me. I *know* how to do this, and I don't want to do it.

Because of this, it's very likely you will quit your website because you're sick and tired of paying someone to make even the tiniest update to it, or you quit your website because you are sick and tired of having to write code every time you want to make an update. Either way, you quit your website, and that is no bueno.

. . .

2. Squarespace: Oh yeah, you're totally right, their sites look amazing... and the search engines hate them. The problem here is that you set up your site, then learn (too late!) that it's actually going to cost more than you thought, and that they throw off a bunch of extraneous code (to make those beautiful background images) that obfuscate the actual *words* on the site (which are what Google looks for), but by then you're in too deep so you have to just live with it. What will end up happening is this: some jerk with a $10 domain and a WordPress installation will outrank you in the search engines, and you will beat your head against a wall because you are overpaying for a website that is practically invisible.

3. Wix—see "Squarespace" above. You probably don't want me to climb back onto that soapbox.

4. "Site Builder" packages offered by hosting companies: Just, no. I don't care how easy the commercial makes the whole process look. This is basically a mashup of two completely different industries (hosting and design/development), and I have never in my 20-plus years in this industry heard anyone say they were thrilled with their site they built with "Blah Blah Hosting Company's Easy Site Building Express package."

In fact, more often than not, I am the person trying to figure out how to back up all the content and move the site off of these other platforms so the client can actually start growing their website and making progress in the search engines.

. . .

There is no need to put yourself at a disadvantage like that when there is such a simple, elegant, low-cost solution available to you in the form of self-hosted WordPress.

What about the free platforms? Can't I just make my website on one of those and call it good?

This topic gets me so fired up, it gets its own section! The answer is, you *can*, but you will regret it. These free sites will eventually find a way to either make money *from* you, or make money *off* of you. By this I mean, if you want to connect your free website to a domain, they're going to charge you. If you want to do anything fancy with the design, they're going to charge you. If you want to hook up email capture so you can build your mailing list (arguably the most important part of doing business online), they're going to charge you.

If they don't make any money charging you for things, they will make money by running ads for other businesses on your website. They will get that money somehow!

"Oh, but I don't want to do any of these things, so I'm good," I hear you saying. Fair enough. But I predict that eventually you *will* want to do one of these things, which is why I am advising you to just pay to take control of your website up-front.

One last reason to not build anything on a free site is because when you put your content on someone else's platform (even if that content is totally original), you are playing by their rules. If they decide you violated their content policy, they can shut down your account (and your website) with no notice at all. I have seen this nightmare scenario happen to writers who built their entire websites on the Blogger platform, only to wake up one morning to find out that Blogger had pulled the plug on their accounts, taking out eight years worth of (not-backed-up) blog posts. Ouch.

You don't need any of those hassles! Just read this guide and spend the time (and the small amount of money) to set things up properly, and you won't end up having to backtrack your way out of situations like these. Since you can buy a domain and a year's worth of hosting for about $30, it's definitely worth the investment.

What If I Get Overwhelmed and Want to Quit?

Listen, I'm not going to lie—this book has A LOT of information in it. Just take it step by step, and you'll totally get there!

To help you work through all of it, I have created a companion guide / workbook where I have boiled this whole book down to something like 50 pages, plus I've given you a bunch of space to take notes. I'm happy to offer you a free printable version of that over at https://loriculwell.com/guide. Seriously, go and grab it!

Okay, time to get started. I hope you're excited! Let's use this momentum to jump right in and get you organized and set up for success!

2
GET YOURSELF ORGANIZED!

I'm going to make this section short, but trust me—*do not skip this step* or you will be mad at yourself later. One of the things I see the most often is people getting super frustrated because there are just so many different services and websites and things to remember in this process, plus enough usernames and passwords to make you really lose your sh*t.

This seems trivial right now, but it can easily get overwhelming and become the reason you either don't finish this process, or don't keep up with it regularly, even if you do. Nothing kills your momentum and enthusiasm like having a great idea for a post, only to lose your inspiration during the 25 minutes it takes you to remember how to log in to your website, change the password, then re-verify it, swearing every step along the way.

I have two solutions for this. First, I recommend starting a brand-new document for all of your website login information. This can be in Word, Excel, or whatever program you prefer. Save this on your desktop and call it "Central Info," or something similarly easy to remember. Then, each time you open an account, go to this document and update it with the name of the company, the email you used to sign up, and all of the login information. Trust me, this is going to come in super handy when you're in the weeds and just about to give up from frustration. I also stuck a password tracker into the printable quick-start guide, which you can grab at https://loriculwell.com/guide

Here are some sample entries:

DOMAIN REGISTRAR:
    (example): namecheap.com
    email:
    username:
    password:

HOSTING COMPANY:
    http://hostgator.com
    username:
    password:

WORDPRESS INSTALLATION:
    https://yourdomain.com/wp-admin
    email:
    username:
    password:

. . .

KEYWORD RESEARCH SOFTWARE:
  www.kwfinder.com
  email:
  password:

Repeat this process for your email list, social media, or any other logins you regularly use for this website or project.

Yes, this seems tedious, but you will absolutely thank me when you need to fix something really quickly on your website and you don't have to spend a half-hour figuring out how to log in. I call this "login fatigue," and after incomplete setup, it's probably the thing that kills the most websites.

I have one other suggestion that can help: If you don't enjoy logging in every single time, you can use a password manager like Dashlane (www.dashlane.com), 1Pass (www.1pass.com), or even Google Password Manager (passwords.google.com). Just be sure to change your passwords frequently, and don't use the same password over and over.

(Yes, I realize that I just said the word "password" so many times, it has ceased to have any meaning for either of us. How do you think I feel?)

Final note: I would highly recommend *not* saving the Central Info document in the cloud, (on, say, Dropbox or in Google Docs). The goal here is to speed up your process when you're working on your website, but you certainly don't want to create a security risk for yourself. (For the record, I never recommend saving passwords anywhere online.)

Also, if you're feeling weird about having all of this info in only one place, it's a great idea to back this document up on an external flash drive, just in case you, say, spill water into your computer (a real-life, painful life lesson, from me to you).

That's it! Great job! Next, let's do some keyword research, so you can get excited about all the demand for your idea!

3
KEYWORD RESEARCH! FUN!

We're going to start this process out by jumping right in and doing some keyword research (because I know how to have a good time).

Look, I'm a writer and SEO nerd by profession and I find keyword research to be an endlessly fascinating snapshot into demand-based marketing, so you'll have to forgive me for suggesting that you do this before you even buy your domain or get started on your project. There is a method to my madness, I promise! You are going to find this interesting! Give it a chance!

The fact is, Google is super competitive about what websites it shows in its search results. Whether you're building a website for a small business or a new idea you're trying to launch, doing a little keyword research at the very beginning can mean the difference between a huge success and a website that will frustrate you because you can never get Google to notice (and rank) it. Also (and you'll have to trust me on this), I have found that people are more motivated to get through the difficult part of the technical setup if they know there is an audience waiting for them on the other side.

If you're already familiar with keyword research and have a go-to software that you like, feel free to use that. If you don't have a preference (and why would you, really? Who am I kidding?), I'm going to suggest that you go over and do the free trial at https://kwfinder.com. This is the keyword tool I use (every single day!), and I honestly think it is one of the simplest, best-designed programs out there. The real key with this tool is that you can see how competitive a word or phrase is, which will give you a huge advantage over everyone else who is making a website. This is super important no matter what kind of website you are setting up. Plus, it's color-coded, which is super nice. Green means go, people!

Here's an example that I hope you like, because it's the scenario I'll be using for the whole book. Let's say you got really into baking sourdough bread during the pandemic, and now you want to start a website where you share your recipes, talk about where you get your starters, do reviews of different bread makers you have tried, and so on. Eventually, you might want to put out a cookbook or add an e-commerce component where you start actually selling the bread.

Great! That is a phenomenal idea, one that you can easily launch quickly and simply, and grow when it catches on.

This is where the keyword research comes in. If you do a little research right now, at the beginning of the process, you will know the following:

1. What domain you should buy (if you don't already have one).

2. What people are searching for (and therefore, what to write about).

3. What specific words and phrases you will want to include in that website so Google will rank your site for them.

Here's how KeywordFinder tells you that. You start with "sourdough" as your search phrase, and the software will return a list of keyword phrases related to the topic, like this one:

☐	reviving sourdough starter from fridge	+243% 710	$0.08	1	
☐	ripe sourdough starter	+26% 640	$0.51	47	
☐	starter for pizza dough	+7% 690	$0.63	42	
☐	sourdough bread starter kit	+904% 44,900	$0.83	100	
☐	purchase sourdough starter	+69% 320	$1.10	100	
☐	frozen sourdough starter	+21% 180	$2.78	89	
☐	sourdough bread making kit	+274% 1,800	$0.89	100	
☐	breadtopia sourdough starter	0% 1,200	$0.89	99	
☐	amish friendship bread starter	+38% 6,300	$0.26	33	
☐	einkorn starter	+55% 150	$0.85	99	
☐	fast sourdough starter	+10% 250	$0.30	75	
☐	sourdough starter maintenance	+50% 790	$0.15	10	
☐	bread machine sourdough starter	+73% 1,300	$0.65	100	
☐	gluten free sour dough	+30% 10,800	$0.90	100	
☐	best flour for sourdough	+114% 4,500	$0.80	100	
☐	best bread flour for sourdough	+114% 4,500	$0.80	100	
☐	sourdough starter culture	+100% 900	$0.70	99	
☐	mature sourdough starter	0% 370	$0.57	94	

Interesting! I don't know a lot about sourdough bread, but I'm assuming each one of these search phrases is a scintillating discussion point in the sourdough community. If you are a sourdough enthusiast, you most likely now have a million ideas for articles, recipes, and interesting things you could talk about on this site—plus you will know what keyword-rich domains would be good to buy if you choose to go that direction with your URL (we'll get there).

As you can see, the software ranks the key phrases by competition. Anything that isn't green is "overly competitive," meaning you're going to have a hard time ranking a brand-new site for that phrase. That's not to say that your site won't rank for those competitive terms eventually, but when you're first starting, you're going to be much more successful if you enter the playing field on minimally competitive phrases to get Google to pick you up right away.

This one search alone will save you a ton of time and the frustration of getting lost in the crowd of people who are trying to rank their websites for more general stuff like "best sourdough recipe." That's going to be really hard!

Another cool thing about this software is that it also shows you the other top-ranking websites for each search phrase, so you can go over and see what they are doing right, get ideas from them, and see who is linking to them.

So, that's my little intro to KWFinder and the reasoning behind why I have people start every project with keyword research. Thank you for hearing me out.

. . .

KWFinder is a paid tool, but you can get a free trial by going to getcreativeinc.com/keywords. If you feel like you're not going to subscribe to the paid tool, be sure to copy (or download) as many lists as you can during the trial period, because you will need them later in this guide.

Great job!

4
THE "WHO WHAT AND WHY" OF YOUR SITE

This is going to sound totally unconventional, but go with me here. Right after you do your keyword research, you are going to have a ton of ideas for content, so I am going to have you just write some stuff for your website right now (even though you don't have your domain or hosting yet). You'll thank me a couple of chapters from now.

The point of this exercise is to strike while the iron is hot, so to speak, because you and I both know that once we get into the nitty-gritty of the technical setup, you're going to be mad at me and in *no mood* to write all the content for your website. So let's do it now and go into this project with a win under our belts, shall we?

Let's do.

. . .

Start by making a folder on your computer called "Website Content." This is where you will start storing things like blog post ideas, the copy for your "About" page, and so on. The more organized you can be now, the easier the setup process will be and the less likely you are to quit.

Who: the target demographic/ ideal user of your website.

Before we do anything on your website, let's take a moment to identify your ideal user. Who are they, exactly? What do they look like? How old are they? What is their level of technical savvy? What are their favorite products? Understanding these things (even in the abstract) will help you make decisions about your website's design and content, ensuring that it aligns with the needs and preferences of those you aim to serve.

It's not useful to say "I want everyone to come to my website and buy my products," because that's almost never true, and it doesn't really help you at all. You actually *don't* want everyone going to your website or buying your products, because when you design for everyone, you design for no one. Ideally, your website or product is mostly for, say, middle-aged women, or single dads, or angsty teenagers. Which one is it? It's fine to have more than one answer, but you do need one primary audience group in mind so you can make some choices. This is your target audience (or you may also hear it referred to as your ideal user, or target demographic).

This will inform how your site is laid out, the features you need to include on it, the design choices you make, your choice of social media platform(s), the tone of your writing, and almost everything else. The better you know your audience, the more successful your site will be.

Back in the old days of the internet and website development, we would spend quality time writing out entire user profiles for people we wanted to use our websites. You may not have the time or desire to do this, so just make sure you have a rough idea of the type of user who is going to come to your site and buy your product. Are they young? Older? Tech-savvy? Not so much? What social media platform do they use the most? Say something about anything!

This seems like a lot of work, and I'm sorry if this is annoying you, because I'm sure what you really want to do is just slap a website together, but this process really helps in terms of long-term strategy. From now on, every piece of content, every word you write, every design choice, and every change you make to the site, you will first consider from the perspective of your ideal user and target demographic.

Target audience: don't make your website without it!

Blog Posts: The "What" of Your Website

Now that we have an idea of your ideal customer/ target demographic, we're going to write some blog posts for them, just to get you used to writing and generating ideas. Pull out your keyword list and take a look at it.

Here's our sourdough keyword list from the last section:

FUNNY YOU SHOULD ASK HOW TO MAKE A WEBSITE 27

☐	reviving sourdough starter from fridge	+243%	710	$0.08	1
☐	ripe sourdough starter	+25%	640	$0.51	47
☐	starter for pizza dough	+7%	690	$0.63	42
☐	sourdough bread starter kit	-304%	44,900	$0.83	100
☐	purchase sourdough starter	+69%	320	$1.10	100
☐	frozen sourdough starter	+21%	180	$2.78	89
☐	sourdough bread making kit	+274%	1,800	$0.89	100
☐	breadtopia sourdough starter	0%	1,200	$0.89	99
☐	amish friendship bread starter	-38%	6,300	$0.26	33
☐	einkorn starter	+55%	150	$0.85	99
☐	fast sourdough starter	+10%	250	$0.30	75
☐	sourdough starter maintenance	+59%	790	$0.15	10
☐	bread machine sourdough starter	+73%	1,300	$0.65	100
☐	gluten free sour dough	+30%	10,800	$0.90	100
☐	best flour for sourdough	+114%	4,500	$0.80	100
☐	best bread flour for sourdough	+114%	4,500	$0.80	100
☐	sourdough starter culture	+100%	900	$0.70	99
☐	mature sourdough starter	0%	370	$0.57	94

. . .

Let's look at this list in terms of website content and let it tell us what the site should be about. I do this by looking over many keyword lists until I have a rough idea of higher-level categories.

A lot of these keyword searches seem like they're going to be recipes, so that's going to be my first category. If the sourdough bread guy (let's call him Steve) had a bunch of recipes lying around, I would advise him to start gathering them up, making sure they are transcribed and easily accessible, and then I'd have him put them in his Website Content folder for the future. I would also have him transfer any sourdough-related photos to this folder, because those are also great for website content and Google ranking.

Reading further down on the list, I see that a lot of people are searching for "buy sourdough starter." As a sourdough expert, Steve probably has many feelings and opinions (and stories of successes and failures) when it comes to sourdough starter. For example, is there a good place to buy it? Do you stockpile it for when you can't find it? Is there a best practice for storing it? He can probably talk for hours (or even days) about just this subject alone, so I would advise him to write these opinions and pieces of expertise down.

The next thing that catches my eye is "sourdough in bread makers."

. . .

As a sourdough expert, Steve probably has a lot of experience when it comes to finding, buying, and using bread makers, and that would make for some interesting posts that could also be affiliate links for product recommendations.

Here are some examples of blog posts I would want Steve to have at the end of this exercise:
 — **How to Buy the Right Bread Maker**
 — **Sourdough Starter for Beginners**
 —-**My Most Successful Recipe: Vegan Sourdough Bread (with Photos!)**

Right now, please take the keyword list for your topic, brainstorm some categories the subjects seem to want to fall into, gather up some content (like ideas and photos), and draft two or three blog posts about your favorite subjects. If you want to do this on actual paper, there is a whole fill-in-the-blank section for that in the free companion guide for this book, available at https://loriculwell.com/guide

About Us/ Welcome: The "Why" of Your Website

After you've written some draft blog posts and you're feeling good about that, you'll immediately move on to creating two other pieces of content that will be useful for your site setup: your "About" page, and your "Welcome" message, where you'll talk about why you're starting this website. These will be similar to each other, so we'll work on them both now.

. . .

The "About" page (which you can also call "About Us" or "About Me" if you want) is important, both to your customers and to Google, because it tells the story of why you're an expert and why people should listen to you. It's good to write your "About" copy when you have a keyword list or two in front of you because a) you can use the keywords in the copy, and b) the keywords will remind you of the nitty-gritty of your subject while you write the "overview" that is the About page.

This copy is usually most effective when it takes the form of a story, like:

Hi, I'm_____, and I am obsessed with all things_____.

Here's why:

The purpose of this website is:

Feel free to take this exact blurb and fill in the blanks/make it your own. For the sourdough bread website, this blurb might look something like:

***

About Me

Hi! I'm Steve, and I am obsessed with all things sourdough! Here's why: when the pandemic started, like many others, I turned my attention to my lifelong love of bread making. I worked my way through starter shortages, different bread makers, and about a thousand recipes (some of which were successful), and eventually found that I loved it so much, I started a small business! Now I make and deliver everything from traditional sourdough bread to cinnamon rolls to my (now famous) vegan sourdough! On this site, I am going to be sharing all of the sourdough insights I've learned —plus I have a book coming out in the fall!

Thanks for visiting, and feel free to get in touch if you have questions or insights about sourdough. I never get tired of learning about my favorite bread! Don't forget to sign up for updates!

***

As you can see, this blurb tells you the story of Steve the sourdough guy, gives you a little context as to why he is such an expert and why you should listen to him. The blurb makes you root for him, and ideally will make you want to follow his website, get on his list, take his recommendations, and buy his book. Off to a great start! Now, because this About blurb won't live on the homepage of your website, I also recommend crafting a short Welcome message which people will see right away. This will be similar in tone to the About message, and can even refer people to that About page if they want to read more. It can look like this:

* * *

Welcome!

I'm Steve, and this is (site name), focusing on <u>recipes</u>, recommendations for things like <u>bread makers</u> and <u>sourdough starters</u>, and my <u>famous vegan sourdough bread</u> and c<u>innamon rolls</u>. Here's some more <u>about me</u> if you're curious.

We have something for everyone at every stage of "sourdough life!" Check out <u>How to Buy the Right Bread Maker</u>, <u>Sourdough for Beginners</u>, and <u>My Most Successful Recipe</u>.

Thanks for visiting, and always feel free to get in touch if you have any questions!

* * *

As I'm sure you surmised, the underlined words represent links to blog posts and pages on the site. These links not only grab the user and pull them into the site, but they also act as internal links for the site, which are good for your search engine optimization (SEO).

And that's it! Look at some keyword lists, gather up some ideas and photos, write some draft blog posts, then write the text for your About page and the Welcome message.

A word to the wise: Definitely do not skip this exercise. The point is to amass as much content as you can for your website now, because a lot of people get writer's block right after the setup (which we'll be doing here very shortly). Head that off at the pass, and write, write, write!

5

ALL ABOUT DOMAINS

Look at us, jumping right in! By the end of this section, you will be able to confidently go out and get a domain (or more than one!). Plus, you're going to be so knowledgeable, you're never going to overpay for a domain ever again.

Let's do this!

Right here, right now, I am going to drop all the latest, greatest knowledge I have when it comes to buying a domain (in the context of this guide, which is websites). That is to say, in this section I am going to walk you through some basic vocabulary about domains, and give you all of my professional knowledge, experience, and opinions when it comes to the art and science of domain buying, *in ord*er to get you out the door with a great domain name for about $10 - $15.

. . .

It can be done!

If you already have a domain (like the name of your business or organization), you can skip this section, although you might want to skim through it for future reference (in case you end up wanting to build a totally new website on another subject later). Once you get the hang of this whole website-building process, you are going to have a million new ideas, so it'll be handy for you to know how to easily get a good domain for a reasonable price.

Oh! One other thing! If you already have a domain, you might be interested to know that you can *transfer* that domain into any registrar you want, meaning you don't have to pay what you've been paying for it. I'm covering stuff like transfers and negotiating premium domains in a little supplementary chapter at the end of this book, so skip to the end if you want to learn about that.

Let's start from the very, very beginning, so we're all on the same page. I am now going to answer some questions and define some terms so we can start strong.

What Is a "Domain"?

Simply put, a domain (also known as a "url" or "web address") is a series of letters and numbers, starting with "http" or "https," that someone will type in or click to get to your website.

It looks like this: www.yourwebsite.com Or www.yourfirstnamelastname.com or www.ILoveBread.com And so on.

. . .

Just so you know (in case you care, and you probably don't), you don't actually "own" your domain. You "register" it with a domain registrar (discussed below) and pay to renew that registration on a yearly basis, kind of like renting a P.O. box where people can send you mail.

That's just a technicality (and probably something you will never have to even consider again), but I told you this guide was going to be thorough, and I meant it, dammit!

What Is a "Registrar"?

Here's another factoid for the "I don't really care" file. We are going deep, people!

A "registrar" is a company that manages the administration of domain names. You will *register* your chosen domain at one of any number of *registrars* in the world.

My go-to domain registrar is NameCheap, which you can find at NameCheap.com, and I'll tell you why. All things being equal, I prefer to pay the least amount possible to register a domain (because I am a domain hoarder and I need professional help).

NameCheap usually has the most competitive price for domains, plus they include free privacy, which is great since I am now recommending that everyone who registers a new domain name also gets the privacy option.

Fun fact: there is no law (or even a rule) that says you have to stay with a certain registrar. If you already have a domain registered somewhere and would like to transfer it over to NameCheap so you can pay approximately $10/year to renew it, you can totally do that!

Maybe you're wondering why you would do this yourself and not have a designer or developer do it for you. Listen up! Even if you are not tech-savvy and want to be hands- off, it is *super* important that all of your stuff is under your control and in your name.

I have seen this particular situation get extremely nasty when a person tries to fire their designer or developer, only to find that the designer/developer actually has their domain and hosting in their own name. Without exaggeration, I once saw a scorned designer charge an author $1,000 to "buy back" her domain (her own name!) from him.

Is stuff like this completely unethical? Absolutely yes. Is it illegal? Nope!

With that kind of situation in mind, do yourself a favor and always, *always* register any domains, and put any and all services, like hosting, social media, and everything else in your own name, with your own credit card, under your own account that is attached to your own email and password. Those things are your property, and they should be treated that way from the beginning.

What is a "Premium Domain"?

If you've ever been searching for a domain and have been (unpleasantly) surprised to find that it's priced in the four-figures (or more), you are in fact already familiar with the concept of the premium domain. "Premium" means that someone else has already registered that domain, but that they are willing to sell it to you for an increased price. I would recommend against this, especially here in the initial setup phase. Right now, you're trying to learn and get something up and running, and you can do that for about $10 - $15 (or less!) at NameCheap.

If you are dying to buy a premium domain, please skip to the bonus material at the end of this guide, where I cover negotiations and escrow. Premium domains are no joke and should be treated as the expensive pieces of real estate that they are. Do not impulse buy a premium domain!

What Are Some Domain-Buying Best Practices?

I could go on and on about this topic, but let me boil it down for you in case you are going to go out and get a domain right this minute. I have longer explanations for why I make these particular suggestions later in this section.

Ideally, your domain will have the following qualities:

— .com, .net, or .org only (no weird extensions)
— Reasonably priced ($10 - $15)
— No hyphens
— Nothing too long, complicated or hard to spell (because people are not as smart as you think)
— No additional add-ons (except privacy)
— Register for one year only
— Do not auto-renew

What is "Privacy"? Why Do I Need It?

"Privacy" simply means that your own name and address will not be connected with that domain name. I used to say privacy didn't matter either way, but since NameCheap offers it for free with every domain, I now wonder why I wasn't using them the whole time.

Let's talk quickly again about what it means to register a domain. When you go to a domain registrar like GoDaddy, NameCheap, or any of the others, you are paying them to become the "manager" of that domain. As part of that management, you agree to have your contact information as the registrant of that domain be publicly available, unless you put privacy on it.

Generally speaking, it is my opinion that you should put your address information out into the world as little as possible, so I always include the privacy option as part of the registration process.

Here are some additional reasons you might want to make the address information private:

1. You are working on a project that might not take off, and you don't want everyone knowing your business.

2. You are working on a project that might become hugely successful, and you don't want everyone knowing your business.

. . .

3. You don't want your address information out there any more than it has to be.

4. If your information is public, people are going to feel free to contact you with inquiries—everything from offering to sell you similar domains to offering you things like hosting and "business opportunities," and you don't need any additional spam email in your life. The bottom line is: definitely get the "privacy" option. It is the only "add on" I recommend when you're buying a domain.

If you're still reading (and why wouldn't you be, really? This level of detail is just super fascinating), let's take my whole domain buying process step by step, so you understand why I made those suggestions and defined all of those terms. Who knows? You might find it interesting!

Our goal here is to get you a great domain that you are excited to build into an actual website, but to do it in a way that is cost-effective enough that you won't be filled with regret if you end up not using it or getting rid of it after a year or two.

Step 1: Brainstorm (Before Going to the Registrar)

The first step in the domain buying process is to decide whether you will focus on your brand/business/idea, or if you want a keyword-rich domain (also known as an "exact match domain" or "EMD" in dumb SEO lingo).

. . .

I will spare you all of the SEO person rhetoric and tell you that the choices are basically this: Are you buying the name of a brand, business, or idea, or are you buying a domain with keywords in it?

Here's the difference: a brand/business domain reflects the name of a brand, business, or idea, whereas a keyword-rich domain is a domain that is made completely out of keywords. The exception to this rule is if you're making a website for a person, in which case the person's name would be the keyword.

I can hear you going, "Duh, that was a totally obvious explanation," so let me tell you why it's important. A domain for a brand, business, or idea will take longer to rank in the search engines because it takes time for search algorithms to figure out what you're trying to do with the site. A domain that is made of keywords will rank faster because it is obvious to the search engines what that site is about, but then you run the risk of over-optimizing it (using way too many keywords).

Example: A website about vegan dessert recipes could be called "Steve's Sweet Life," and it might have a domain like stevessweetlife.com, or it could be called "Vegan Dessert Ideas," with the domain vegandessertideas.com.

The very latest thinking about which one is better is this: if you intend to pursue a more long-term SEO strategy with your website, it is safer to get the "brand name" domain. This is not a book about SEO so I don't want to get us too sidetracked here, but when in doubt, go with a "brand name." It will take longer to rank, but you won't have to watch yourself when you're doing your search engine optimization. The way to decide is to ask yourself if this is a long-term site or a "one and done" project that you're not really going to keep adding to. If it's the latter, you're fine going with an exact match.

The best practices for actually choosing a domain (exact match or not) are all the same, so just follow the example below and it will all make sense. The main point of this step is for you to brainstorm before you actually go over to a registrar, because if you are not clear on what you want or need, you will overpay and buy a lot of domains you will not end up using. Trust me on this!

Step 2: Search, Narrow Down, and Decide!

Okay, let's now go over to NameCheap and run some searches. We are doing this example with exact match keywords, because I'm assuming the fictional sourdough bread guy is not going to be that into a long-term SEO strategy so he's not going to be continually adding keyword-rich content to this site. Also, I'm sure this is totally obvious, but if you are building a website/brand based on a made-up word, that domain will probably be available so you won't need to do any of the negotiating part.

Here's a quick search on "sourdough bread":

FUNNY YOU SHOULD ASK HOW TO MAKE A WEBSITE

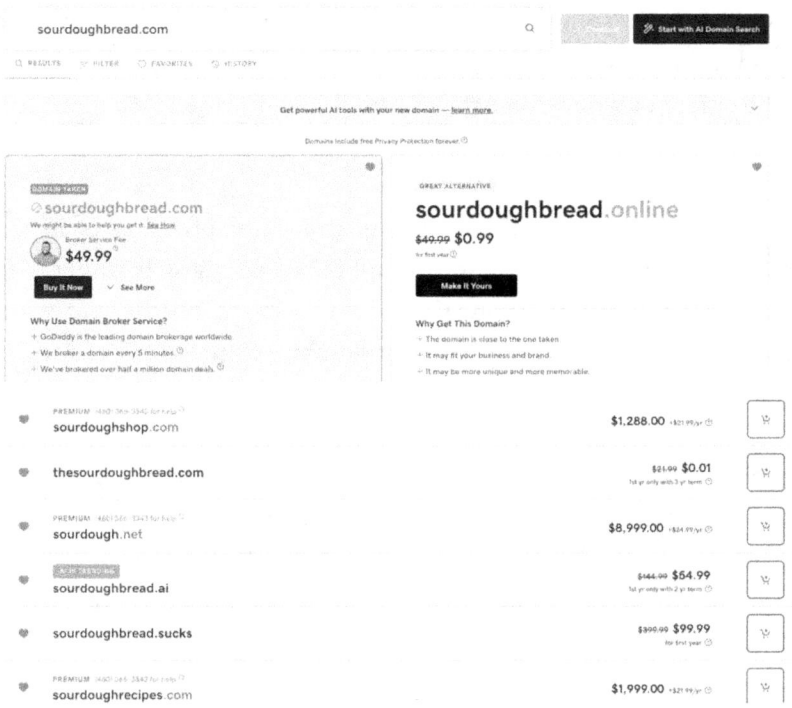

Wow! This is nuts. I don't mind saying I am super surprised at the value of a sourdough-specific domain!

As you can see, someone already owns sourdoughbread.com, but the domain registrar is happy to charge you $4.99 to send an email to the current owner to see if they would want to sell it to you.

No, thank you! Generally speaking, this kind of thing is just a complete waste of money. SourdoughBread.com guy is unlikely to even answer that email, but if he does, rest assured he will want tens of thousands of dollars for that domain. Nope!

My next move is to look at the .net and .org versions of domains, but those are also premium and/ or unavailable, so I would recommend skipping those as well. Sourdoughrecipes.com is also premium and would limit what you could talk about on the site.

I'm not crazy about any of the "all extensions" suggestions because honestly, I just do not think people are smart enough to understand that something like sourdoughdoughbread.online is an actual website.

Because I am trying to be helpful to you, I looked through 400 mostly stupid derivative domain extensions and pulled out some I would actually buy. At this point, with all of the available information (and let me stress that I would *not* recommend going back and forth on this decision for days or weeks), I would recommend you go with one of the following:
    thesourdoughbread.com

sourdoughbreadpro.com
sourdoughbreadonline.com

Any one of these fine domains fulfills all of my criteria—they are inexpensive ($10 - $15 apiece!), end in a .com, and contain the main keyword phrase that you want the site to rank for.

Side note: If this niche interests you and you want to buy one of them and follow along, any and all of these domains are still available and can be registered at NameCheap for about $9. Buy one, build it out, and let me know how it goes!

Second side note: before you buy a domain, always, always run the phrase through a simple trademark check just to make 100% sure you are allowed to use that phrase. I have put a link to the US Government Trademark checking website over at: getcreativeinc.com/check

Step 3: Run the Registration Gauntlet, Say No to Almost Everything

We're moving now, right? In this theoretical example, I have narrowed down my options, decided on thesourdoughbread.com, and have added it to my cart. That looks like this:

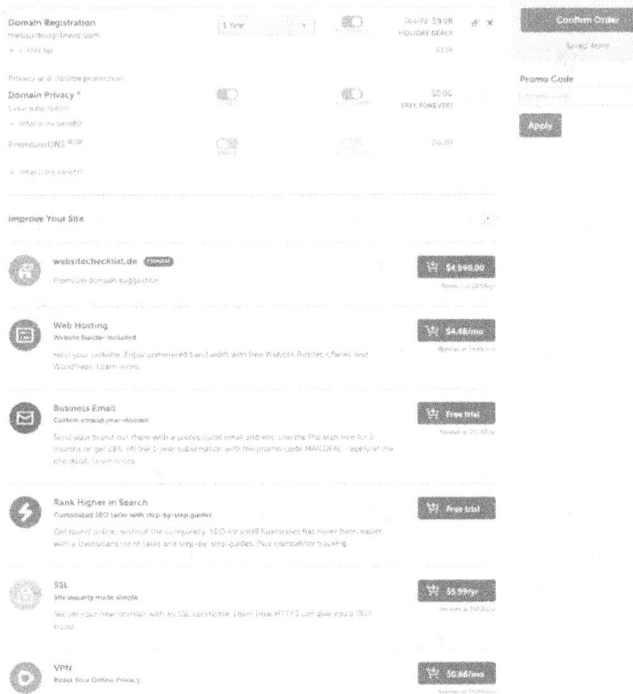

. . .

Now I will answer all of the questions I know you have by "nope-ing" my way down this a of "frequently recommended" offers and suggestions. This is the registrar trying to get you to spend more money, but a lot of this stuff is unnecessary, so don't give in!

1. Web Hosting: NOPE! You are eventually going to need some hosting, but if you buy it now, you are going to overpay. There are much better deals to be had, and we will find some in the very next chapter.

2. SSL: NOPE! This will be included with your hosting account, or you can get this for free at Cloudflare.com. Buying it here is unnecessary.

3. Professional email: NOPE! This will also be included with your hosting.

4. VPN: NOPE! This is some next-level tech stuff that you will most likely never need, and if you do need it, there are better places to get it. Honestly, I do not even know why they offer this as an add-on.

5. WordPress hosting: NOPE! This is just for *one* website, but the hosting I recommend supports multiple WordPress installations. If you'll notice, this is the most expensive add-on, and that is because they know it's a little complicated, and people are intimi-

dated by this process. You do not need to pay $22.88/year *per website* for something I will teach you in this guide!

6. The .net, .org, .tv, and .dev versions of the same domain: NOPE. You do not need multiple versions of the same domain right at this moment. My best-practice rule is to pick one of these extensions, build that up, then go back for the rest if the first one takes off. Right here is where I will also mention how people always say to me, "Well, I'll just buy all of the extensions so no one else takes them."

This is when I say: "*Who would take them?*" They're all right there and they're super affordable, so if someone were going to snap them up, they would have done that already (and they would be attempting to overcharge you for them). I'm not a betting person, but if I were, I'd bet in a year that they'll still be there, right where you left them. If your website/idea takes off and gets $100 million in venture capital, rest assured that you will be able to have your high-powered legal team go through and buy up every single instance of this domain name.

Here are some more screenshots of "offers" that I feel like I need to make fun of:

thesourdoughbread.xyz	$1.48/yr Retail $13.98/yr	Add to cart
thesourdoughbread.tech	$34.99/yr Retail $61.98/yr	Add to cart
thesourdoughbread.me	$7.98/yr Retail $18.98/yr	Add to cart
thesourdoughbread.info	$3.48/yr Retail $21.98/yr	Add to cart
thesourdoughbread.pro	$2.98/yr Retail $21.93/yr	Add to cart
thesourdoughbread.live	$3.48/yr Retail $29.98/yr	Add to cart
thesourdoughbread.art	$1.98/yr Retail $25.98/yr	Add to cart
thesourdoughbread.ink	$2.98/yr Retail $24.98/yr	Add to cart
thesourdoughbread.is	$45.98 Renews at $47.98/yr	Add to cart
thesourdoughbread.cc	$5.98/yr Retail $10.98/yr	Add to cart
thesourdoughbread.so	$64.98/yr	Add to cart
thesourdoughbread.ac	$28.98/yr Retail $32.98/yr	Add to cart
thesourdoughbread.cx	$19.98/yr	Add to cart
thesourdoughbread.sh	$34.98/yr Retail $38.98/yr	Add to cart

. . .

This is when the whole domain industry goes truly "absurdist theater" to me. What even are some of these extensions? Have you ever heard of a good website with one of these? Better yet, can you imagine saying to someone "Oh yeah—go check out my website! It's thesourdoughbread.lol, or thesourdoughbread.baby"? Just. No.

Also, if you are about to say "Oh, I'm just going to buy all of those extensions and redirect them over to the .com version," please let me encourage you to just go ahead and take a $10 bill for each of the domains you're going to do that for and just throw it right in the garbage (or light it on fire if that's more your thing). Because let me assure you, there is *no value whatsoever* in redirecting a domain with a weird extension that has never been owned or developed and therefore has no traffic (power) behind it.

Google doesn't even know about these weird domains, so Google does not give a single crap if you redirect them over to the .com. The only entity that will be happy/benefit from you redirecting your ".baby" extension is the domain registrar, and they are not even going to say thank you for that free money you just gave them.

My bottom line is this: These weird extensions, while hilarious, are a straight-up waste of money that benefit only the registrar and no one else. They are one of the biggest cash grabs out there, and it baffles me that they are presented in a way that is so convincing, I have often had to argue with clients to talk them out of buying them.

. . .

Clearly, I have feelings. The bottom line is, do not add any of these things right now. Remember, you are trying to get out of here for just the price of the domain.

Here is the next-to-last screen in the registration process:

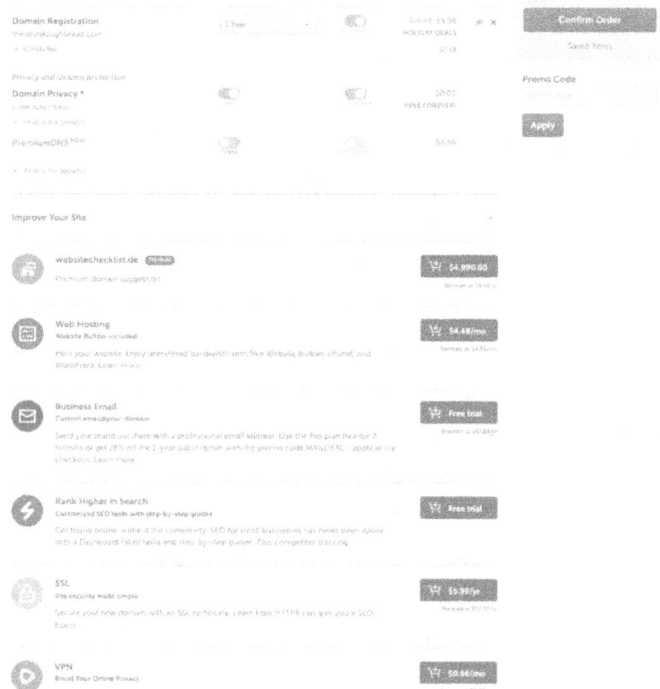

As you can see, NameCheap includes the privacy for free. Privacy is the *only* add-on I recommend, so if your registrar offers it (even if they charge), definitely add it.

Another thing I'm going to point out is that you will also be given the option to register the domain for anywhere from one to 10 years.

Always go with one year, maximum two if they offer you a killer deal. *Do not* pre-pay for ten years, no matter what they offer you. There is almost no scenario where I would recommend pre-paying for ten years. Do I believe in your idea? Of course! Do I want you to be stuck paying for a sourdough bread domain for ten years if you somehow wind up discovering you're gluten-intolerant?

No, I do not.

I also would not recommend auto-renewing, so I have unchecked that button. I have rarely been excited to see an email from a registrar that a domain auto-renewed.

As you can also see, NameCheap is going to offer me those options I already "noped" on the last screen, perhaps to confuse and disorient me. I am going to once again NOPE! all of these choices. I also do not want PremiumDNS, which is a sort of domain monitoring service that you might want to add later if your site blows up. Right now, you are at the beginning of the process, so frankly, it is highly unlikely that someone is going to come along and try to steal your domain (no offense. You're great!)

And that's it! You have a headache and you're probably sweating, but you found a domain, registered it, and confidently got out of there *for like ten dollars. Go*, you!

Step 4: Put Your Info Into That Spreadsheet

Look at me, already referring back to something I just established three chapters ago!

Once you register your domain, NameCheap (or whatever registrar you used) is going to send you a confirmation email. Right now, before you forget, go over to that Excel spreadsheet I mentioned in Chapter 2 and write down all the information about this domain, including the name of the registrar, the username/password, the date you registered it, and any other information that is going to be useful to you for reference purposes. You'll need to know how to log in so you can make changes to the domain.

That is pretty much it for domain buying. I have also put some (totally optional) bonus material at the end of the book, just for brand domains, domain transfers, and negotiating for premium domains if you have your heart set on one of those.

Right now, let's move on to hosting!

6
GET SOME HOSTING!

That last section was *a lot*. Believe me, I know. I hope you've recovered appropriately because now we're moving on to hosting.

Can I recommend you take a walk or have a drink before you continue?

No? Fine. You know yourself best. Let's keep going.

Okay! So, you've got your domain (or domains), and you're excited to move on to the next step, which is buying a hosting plan where you'll put your website (or websites).

What is happening here?

. . .

Just so you can get your head around what we're doing, in this section, I am explaining how and why you want shared hosting that 1) can hold more than one website, and 2) does not already have WordPress installed. This combination is perhaps the best kept secret in the personal website industry. Yes, this is going to get a little technical at times, but please stick with me, because this method is going to save you SO MUCH MONEY.

Seriously. I believe in it enough to hit you with the "all caps" there, so you know it's going to be good.

First of All, What Exactly *Is* "Hosting?"

Simply put, your "host," or hosting company, is the space that holds your website so it comes up when people go to your domain. You need both a domain (website address) *and* hosting (space) for the website to actually appear when people type that domain into a browser window.

Wait—did I just tell you that you're going to be renting "space"? Didn't I promise this was going to be an easy-to-understand guide?

I did. Don't overthink it. You need a domain and some hosting to put it on. That's really the bottom line.

Basically, you need hosting to have a website. *However*, you do not have to pay too much for that hosting, and you *certainly* do not have to pay a web developer or designer for it. Shared website hosting (which is what we're going to be getting you here) should run you about $5 - $10 per month, and that is for *multiple* websites (because once you get the hang of this process, you are for sure going to have more ideas and make more than one).

What Hosting Company is the Best?

I'm going to walk you through getting hosting from a couple of different companies because once you learn what you're looking for, you can pretty much get it anywhere.

What I would advise is that you read through these examples, take the best-practices list, and visit several of the hosting companies I have linked at the end of this chapter.

Hosting companies are just like any other company—they regularly have sales and deals, especially around holidays and events. When you're trying to decide on hosting, definitely compare the different companies to see which one has the best deal, and if you're not in a hurry, wait for a holiday sale! One stealthy way to do this is to sign up for the email lists of all the hosting companies I list at the end of this section, then wait for them to start sending you offers and discounts. It won't take long, and you'll end up with some great deals!

I'm going to jump in and start telling you what I would recommend buying where, but if you're not quite ready just yet, bookmark this section and get it out again when you're ready to pull the trigger. This is going to get specific!

NameCheap Hosting

First, I'm going to cover NameCheap, because that's where I recommended you get your domain, and it's *slightly* easier to connect your domain to your hosting when they're in the same place. The only thing I don't love about NameCheap is that their support is chat-only, so if you get stuck, you can't call them and have them walk you through things. Phone support is one of my must-have recommendations for hosting, but as I mentioned, the setup is easier if you have both domain and hosting in the same place, plus I have found their chat-based tech support to be excellent, so I would still recommend them. This scenario presupposes the fact that you already have a domain at NameCheap or are planning on getting one there, so if that is NOT the case for you, just keep in mind that your process might look a little different. The mechanics are mostly the same, so I'm starting with the NameCheap example and building from there.

The type of hosting you want is called "shared," meaning you are paying the hosting company for a little bit of space on their very large server. This is totally safe, and you will not feel like you are sharing space at any time.

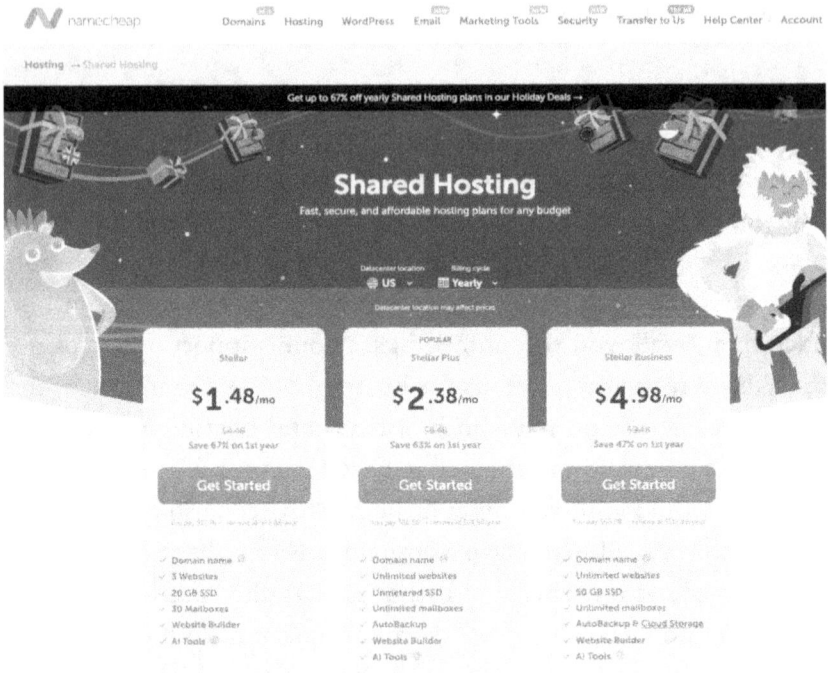

In case you're curious (which again, I'm sure you aren't, but I'm trying to be thorough here), there are several reasons why you want this particular shared hosting and not any of the other choices you will be offered (which I will cover now if you're interested).

Hosting You Don't Want

You're welcome to skip over this section if you don't care, but some people want me to explain *why* I am advising them to say no to things, so here you go:

1. WordPress Hosting—As I mentioned in the chapter on domains, you don't want WordPress hosting, because that product is charging you a premium for *doing* the WordPress installation. This

guide is going to teach you how to do that yourself, so you don't want to limit yourself from the very beginning. Save that money and reinvest it in something like design or advertising! The only time I would recommend this type of hosting is if you know for absolute certain that you're not going to want to do the setup and maintenance of WordPress yourself. I'm pretty sure you wouldn't be reading this guide if that were the case, but if that describes you, skip to "WordPress Hosting" at the end of this section and go with that!

2. Reseller Hosting—Honestly, I do not know why hosting companies include this in their list of regular choices. Reseller hosting is for web professionals who are going to sell hosting to their clients, and if you were going to do that, you would already know what your choices were for that offering. Do not give this another thought.

3. VPS Hosting—Again, no. This is mostly for developers, and it is much more space than you need for what you're going to be doing with your website (or websites).

4. Dedicated Server—No! Also for developers and web professionals. If and when you end up needing a VPS or a dedicated server, you will know it and you'll need to do a lot more due diligence to choose the environment that is right for you. Now is not the time for that.

Bottom line: Regular shared hosting is going to be your best deal at this moment. We will now move on to which plan to choose! Here are the offerings over at NameCheap under Shared Hosting. My recommendation is always to get the equivalent of the middle level of hosting, which at NameCheap looks like this and is called Stellar Plus. I have x'ed out the one I don't recommend and circled my preference using my truly rudimentary Photoshop skills:

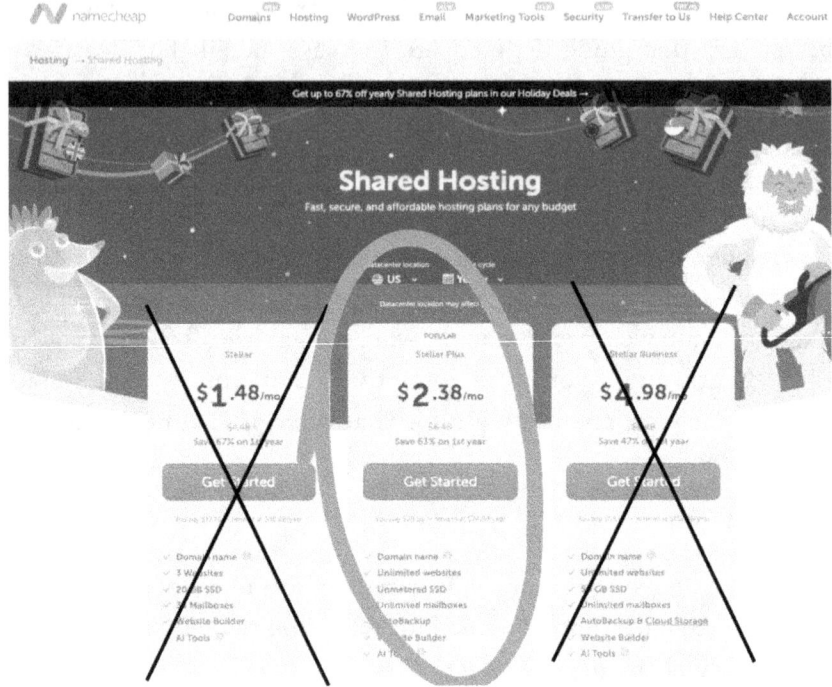

You're welcome to get the Stellar Business version if that's what you would prefer (it has more storage and better backup), but don't go lower than Stellar Plus because, as you can see, the Stellar plan only allows for three websites, whereas Stellar Plus holds an unlimited amount. You also get unmetered bandwidth and auto-backup with that plan.

At the time I took this screenshot, NameCheap was running a deal to save 45% on the first year, which is great. Two-plus years is also a good deal, but I will warn you that NameCheap has a little bit of a gotcha charge hidden in the fine print of their hosting—they make you pay for your SSL certificate after the first year. Instead of even setting that up, just set up a free account on CloudFare.com and run your NameCheap-hosted site through there for the free SSL Cert. Simple!

Side note: even if you love this book and decide to become a website developer, I would not recommend putting 100 websites on a shared hosting account (for reasons I will cover in the FAQ portion of this section), but I do like the freedom it gives you when you're first starting out.

Okay, so you've chosen Stellar Plus, and you're ready to move on. Let's run the checkout gauntlet together so I can tell you what to avoid!

On this screen, NameCheap is going to need to know what domain you want connected to this hosting account. If you already went through the domain-buying process with them in the last chapter, you'll select "existing domain name," log in to your account, and pick one of the domains you bought. (If you only bought one, your choice is clear!)

NameCheap also gives you the opportunity to set a third-party domain as the primary domain for this hosting account, so if your domain lives somewhere else at the moment, that's still okay (although I do think you should transfer it eventually and save yourself some money).

. . .

The final thing you will see is the shopping cart, where you will basically be offered all of the same things as when you bought your domain. That looks like this:

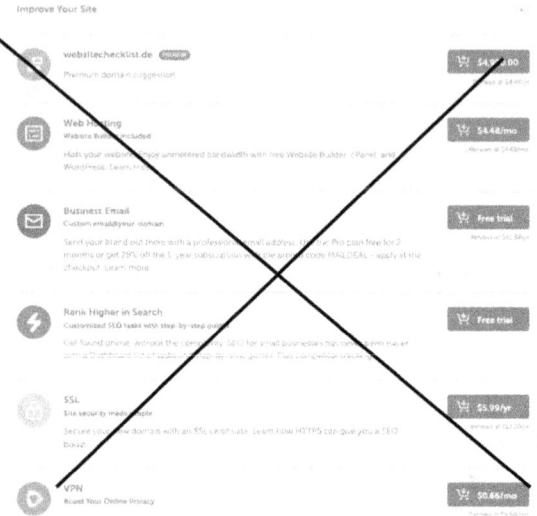

You still do not need any of these add-ons. You'll be able to establish email accounts for this domain, install the security certificate, and perform backups yourself, just from the cPanel of your shared hosting account. These add-ons are basically just trying to make it easier for you to find these things.

You don't need that. You're tough! You made it this far! Also, if you find that you absolutely do need one of these things, believe me, NameCheap will be only too happy to sell one or all of them to you, any time of the day or night.

For now, just check out, and when you get your confirmation email with all of your hosting details, go back into your Central Info document and write down absolutely everything about this hosting account, including your username, password, and the name servers they send you. You will for sure be referring to all of this information later, so write it all down when you get it!

If you got both your domain and hosting from NameCheap, you're done! You can skip to the next chapter.

If you want to shop around and buy hosting somewhere else (which I totally get—I love a bargain!), here are a few more examples of what that looks like at other hosting companies.

HostGator
    http://hostgator.com
    Over at HostGator (another company I use and recommend), the shared hosting plan I recommend is called the "Baby Plan," and looks like this:

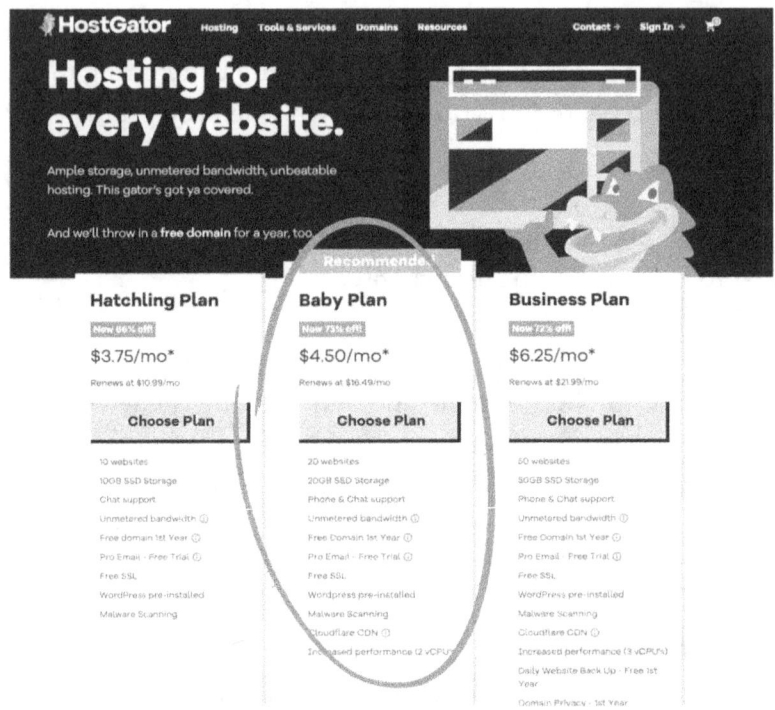

As I mentioned with NameCheap, you can feel free to go one level *up* with this hosting and get the "Business Plan," which has a few more features, but I would not recommend going down to the "Hatchling Plan," because that single-website limit is going to really inhibit your growth and frustrate you.

HostGator is a great choice because they have call-in tech support, plus they regularly offer killer deals on hosting. The one and only offer I would not recommend you take them up on is the free domain, which they will try to give you when you sign up for hosting.

The reason I would turn this down is because the privacy (which, if you'll recall, is the only add-on I recommend when you're buying a domain) is $14.95/year. Also, HostGator is going to offer to give you this domain for free (plus that fee for the privacy) for one year, but then they're going to try to charge you about $13 (plus privacy) to renew that domain.

NameCheap offers domain registration with free privacy for less than the cost of the privacy at HostGator, so I recommend skipping their offer, picking the "I Already Own This Domain" option, and using your NameCheap domain as the main domain for your hosting account.

Choose the "Baby" or "Business" plans (as I mentioned above) and enter your billing information.

Here are some other things you do *not* need when you are checking out (no matter which hosting company you go with):

—Extra SSL certificate. NOPE! A security certificate comes with the hosting account. You do not need an extra one.
　—Extra security. NOPE! There are WordPress plugins for this, and if you install one or more of those and you're still not satisfied, you can always upgrade after the fact.
　—Extra email accounts. NOPE! You will be able to access your email from the cPanel of your hosting account.
　—Backups. NOPE! There are WordPress plugins for this, and again, if you don't like any of those, you can add the backup service with the hosting company at a later date.
　—SEO Tools. NOPE! There is a WordPress plugin for this, plus I am going to give you a killer SEO strategy later in this guide.

. . .

That's it! You simply hit "check out," receive your hosting details in your email, and then enter that information into your Central Info document.

I'm sure you get the point, but I will do this process one additional time for BlueHost (another company I use, like, and recommend).

BlueHost

http://bluehost.com

As with the other examples, you want the "Plus" or "Choice Plus" level of the "Shared Hosting," not the entry-level or pro accounts, and you want that for one or two years (unless you are buying hosting for a business or personal website that you know is still going to be around in three years). Get the best deal you can!

As you can see, in this case, BlueHost's prices do not compare to NameCheap or HostGator's, but I am including this example because it never hurts to look around!

One thing I like about BlueHost is that they offer 24/7 live call-in tech support, which is nice if you get stuck in the middle of the night and need that one-on-one help.

The next step with BlueHost is to establish that domain, and although BlueHost will want you to either register a new domain or establish a domain that you already have (like with Name-Cheap), or they will give you the option to skip this step and set this up later, which is handy.

Like HostGator, BlueHost will give you the domain for free, but they will charge you for domain privacy. They get approximately $12/year for this, but again, NameCheap is still less and includes free privacy, so I would recommend just turning down the free BlueHost domain.

Like the other options, I would recommend un-checking all the "package extras," because everything they are offering can be accomplished on the cPanel or with plugins.

That's it for BlueHost! Just save the registration details and the name servers in your Central Info doc, and you're good to go.

. . .

Since I have now done this example three different times with different hosting companies, I'm going to assume that you get the point and that it'd be redundant for me to go through it again. Moving on!

WordPress Hosting

If you skipped to this section because you know for a fact you're not going to want to do the WordPress installation and security updates yourself, and you're fine paying the premium monthly fee, great! I would still recommend going with the mid-range or higher plan for any hosting company you're going to use, just because you get more benefits at that range. WordPress hosting is still pretty new, so every company is going to offer different stuff, all of which I will go over in this list to try to help you make your decision.

I'm going to cover these in the order in which I would recommend them.

HostGator

HostGator's WordPress hosting is the best-priced one I could find, and some of their plans allow you to have multiple domains. I would go with "Standard" or "Business," because that would give you two or three sites (respectively) and make it more worth the money.

NameCheap

Here is the "WordPress Hosting" at NameCheap: https://www.namecheap.com/wordpress/ As you can see, this is approximately $8/month for one website, but they do the setup for you and give you a lot of space, plus some extras.

BlueHost

BlueHost was the first "traditional" hosting company to come out with one of these really premium-priced offers, so I'm showing it to you as an example. Any of these plans will include the WordPress installation and some extra security, and will be fine for your needs. Remember, these prices are for **one website per month:**

WP Engine

https://wpengine.com

Finally, if you're really don't mind paying more for premium hosting services, definitely check out WP Engine. They're basically the industry standard for WordPress hosting:

That's it for hosting! I keep an even longer and more obsessive list of hosting companies over at https://getcreativeinc.com/hosting in case that interests you.

. . .

Remember: mid-range plan, bring your own domain, make sure it includes a free SSL cert, no add-ons, and get the best price.

Oh! And as always, if you have questions about hosting companies you think I should expand upon, please let me know!

7
CONNECT DOMAIN WITH HOSTING

Great job! You're taking this step by step. I hope you're not feeling too overwhelmed; or if you are, I hope you'll take a break before continuing, so you can resist the urge to throw this book across the room (or whatever the equivalent is with an ebook).

The next step in the setup process is to connect your domain with the hosting you just bought. This varies a bit by company, but I'll give you the basics, and if you get stuck, absolutely call (or chat with) your chosen companies to have them walk you through this part.

We'll go through this example twice—once where the domain and hosting are both at NameCheap, and once where the domain is at NameCheap but the hosting is somewhere else.

. . .

If you are using another registrar, that's totally fine! The concepts will still apply, but the elements will likely be located in different places and called different things. Take advantage of whatever customer service that company offers!

The big picture of what you're doing here is simple: you are pointing your domain toward the space you bought at the hosting company, so your website shows up when someone types it in.

Example 1: NameCheap Domain + Hosting

Log in to your NameCheap account, then click the "Domain List" button. That's this one:

You will then be taken to a list of all of your domains (which might only be one if you've just started).

Remember that step in the hosting section where you were asked to associate a domain with the hosting account?

No? Go back to that section really quickly.

Got it? Okay. This is the moment. NameCheap might have done this for you already, and if they did, great!

FUNNY YOU SHOULD ASK HOW TO MAKE A WEBSITE   81

. . .

If not, this is the missed step that is going to end up in tears and multiple late-night tech support chats, my friends. Do not skip it!

Find the domain you want to associate with this hosting account, then click the little "Manage" button to the right of it. When you click the "Manage" button, the next screen is basically all the settings for the domain.

What you're looking for is this box right here, which is the equivalent of the "address" field. This is telling the domain where to look for the website that is attached to it.

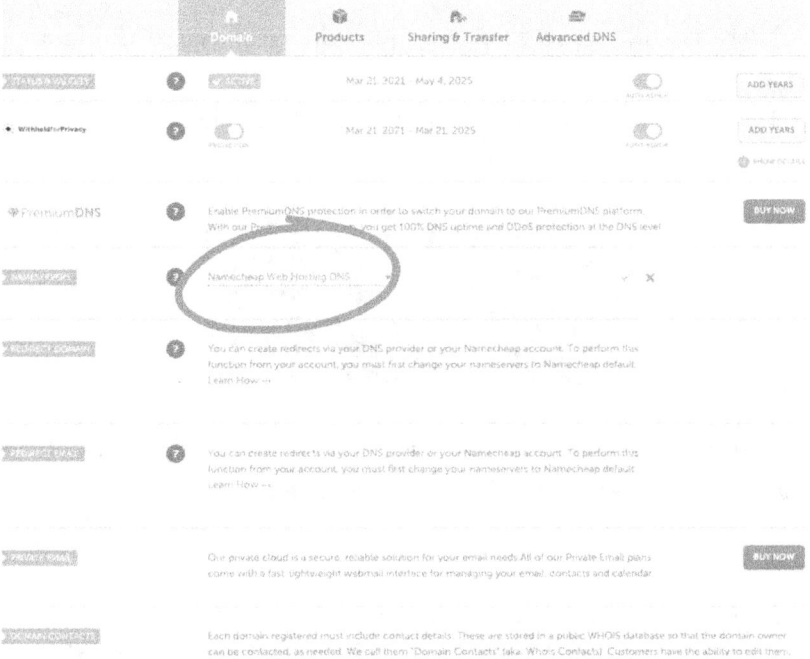

If you got your hosting from NameCheap, switch this to "NameCheap Web Hosting DNS," then click the little checkbox to confirm your choice.

After you make this change, it still might take a little while to "propagate." It usually happens pretty fast, but it can take 24-48 hours.

If you got both your domain and hosting from NameCheap, you're done! Skip to the next chapter (installing WordPress).

Example 2: NameCheap Domain + Outside Hosting

OK, here is that same example, but when we get to the "name server" step, we do something else.

Log in to your NameCheap account, then click the "Domain List" button. That's this one:

You will then be taken to a list of all of your domains (which might just be one if you've just gotten started).

Find the domain you want to associate with this hosting account, then click the little "Manage" button to the right of it. That looks like this:

FUNNY YOU SHOULD ASK HOW TO MAKE A WEBSITE 83

When you click the "Manage" button, the next screen is basically all the settings for the domain.

What you're looking for is this box right here, which is the equivalent of the "address" field.

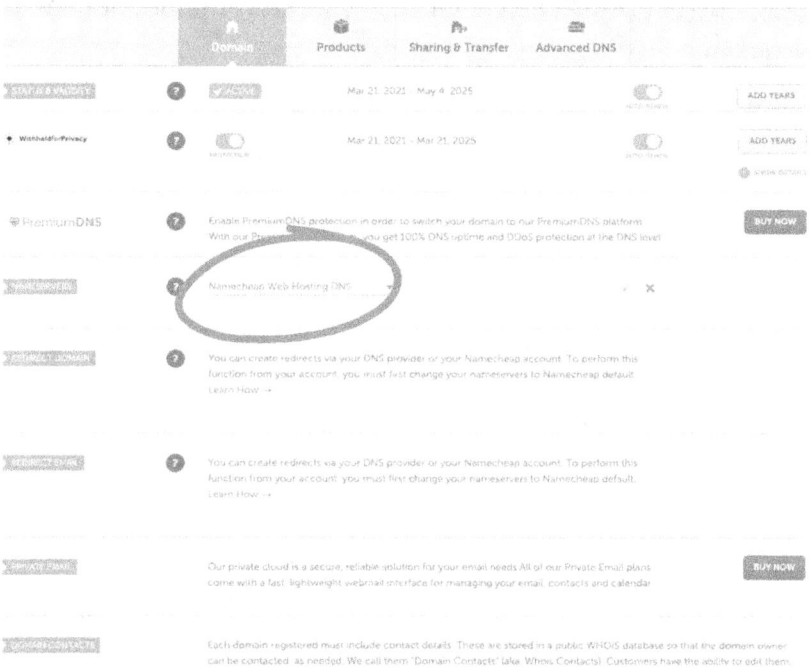

In this case, instead of telling NameCheap to look internally for your hosting, we are going to give it another "address" where your website hosting lives.

Stick with me! We're almost done!

. . .

Remember that part in the "Hosting" section where the hosting company sent you a confirmation email with your account details, and I recommended saving that information in a "Central Info" document so you could easily find it later?

This is later. Go and get that information.

Click "Custom DNS," then enter the name server information into the boxes.

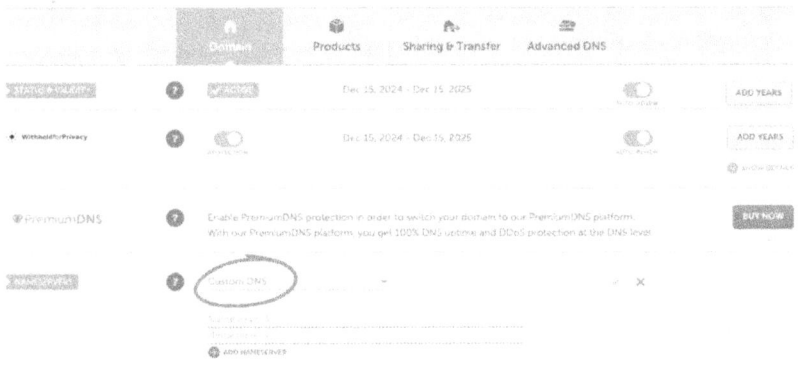

Go ahead, stop for a second to swear at me if it helps. :)

Once you have those filled in, check the (sometimes hard to find) little blue checkbox on the right to confirm, and you're done!

. . .

Your part is complete! You will have to wait a little while (maximum 24-48 hours) for this change to take effect, since things are being connected on the back-end. This has nothing to do with you, and now is a good time for you to take a break!

Great job! I know, that was kind of terrible, but you are going to save *so much money* when you don't have to ask a tech person to do this for you!

8

INSTALL WORDPRESS

First off, you might not even need this section right now! If you chose "WordPress Hosting," or if your hosting company included "WordPress installation" as part of their setup process, you're good!

You would know that because the hosting company would have walked you through it at some point, then you would have gotten a confirmation email with your login details.

No? Okay, just checking.

There are only two things to do in this section: find your cPanel access and actually install the WordPress software onto your domain. Let's get started!

. . .

First: Find the cPanel

I'm assuming you have allowed enough time since the last step to let the domain + hosting change propagate, so the very next thing you'll do is log in to your hosting account (have that "Central Info" document handy at all times!) and make your way to the cPanel for your hosting. cPanel is short for control panel, and it's the place where you can do all the website things.

If you are using a different hosting company, that's completely fine! Just read my NameCheap example and try to find the equivalent in your chosen hosting company. Do not panic!

Getting to the cPanel will look a little different depending on the hosting company you chose. In NameCheap, you're looking for the "Hosting List" button in the main navigation, which looks like this:

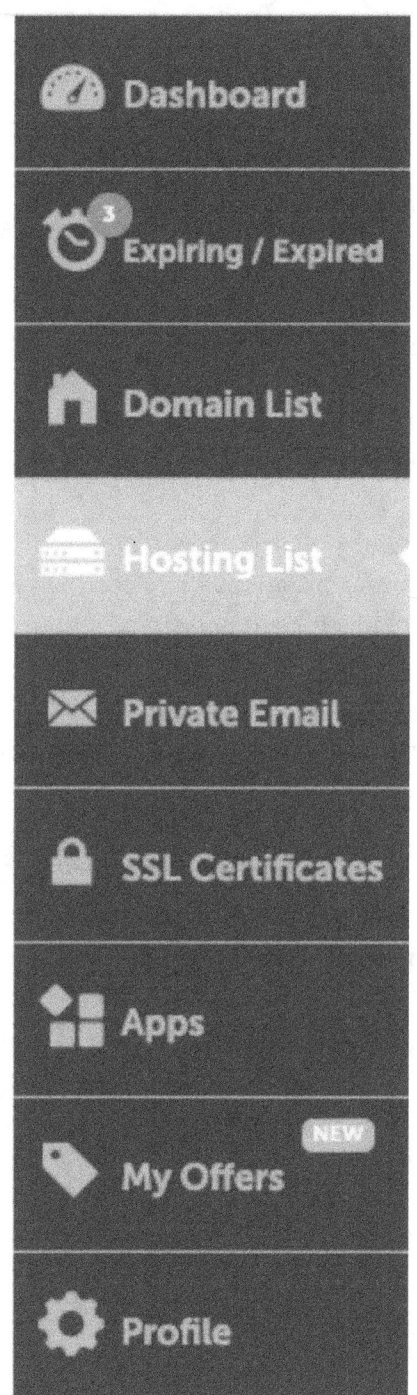

Once you click that, you'll see this:

Hosting Subscriptions					
Subscription	Plan	Status	Auto-Renew	Expiration	
	Stellar Business			Aug 31, 2026	GO TO CPANEL

Click the "Go to cPanel" button!

2. Install WordPress

Are you feeling super productive and tech-savvy? You should be, because you are killing it right now!

Seriously, many people are crying by this point or have broken something. But you're so close!

Once you're in the cPanel (which looks the same no matter what hosting company you're using), you'll scroll down until you see this logo:

Click it, and you'll see this screen:

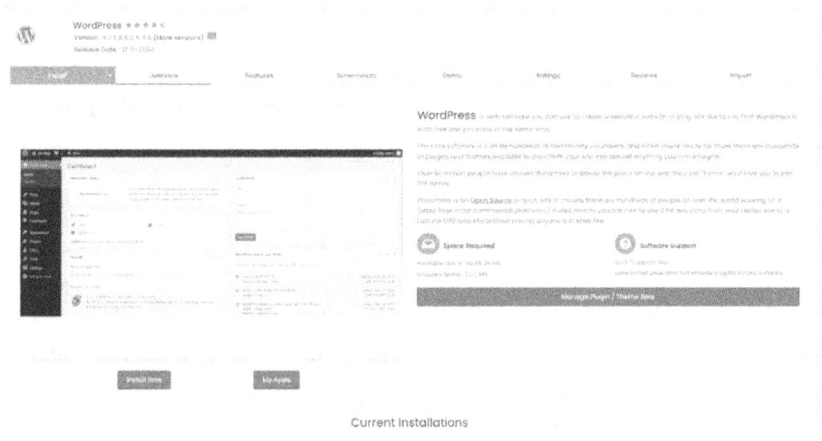

Click "Install Now," then select the domain on which you want to install the WordPress software. Since you only have one domain so far, there will only be one choice.

MAKE SURE THIS BOX IS BLANK OR YOU WILL BE SORRY:

In Directory ⓘ

Yes, that was an all-caps moment. You want the installation on the **root of the domain**, not in a directory folder. If this box is not blank, your website will end up appearing in a weird place on your domain. This will frustrate and outrage you and cause you to break things. As far as I can tell, almost every hosting company has caught on to this and is just directing you to put your WordPress installation right onto the root, which is what they should have been doing all along.

However, a few hosts still default to suggesting that you install into the /wp folder, which is just going to end in that frustrating moment when you realize that you've built an entire website into that one folder and will now need to redirect everything over there or migrate the whole thing into the root. SAVE YOURSELF THE HASSLE. Write yourself a note that says, "Erase the /wp folder."

You laugh now, but believe me, this one point is going to save you hundreds of hours.

. . .

There may also be a slight delay while your hosting company installs the security certificate. If this is the case, take a break (because we all know you could use one), and then come back and finish the installation.

At this point, you're basically just trying to get out of this section as quickly as possible. The goal is to just get the bare-bones installation of the WordPress software on the domain, and if you stop to overthink about themes and plugins, this will never happen. For that reason, here is what I advise:

- Fill out all of the required information, *but do not overthink it* because you can change everything later. Be sure to save the password because you will need it to log in, and it is annoyingly difficult to change if you can't log in.

- Change your installation username to something other than "admin." (Leaving it as "admin" is a good way to get hacked.)

- Make sure you put your email in the "Email installation details to" box.

- Hit "Install."

You will receive an email with the details of your WordPress installation. Take all of the information in that email and put it immediately into your "Central Info" document. You will need this information to log in to your website so you can edit it.

. . .

That's it! Surprisingly easy, right?

I'm joking. I know that was kind of the worst.

Believe it or not, your website is actually "live" now, meaning you can visit it on the internet. Of course, you'll need to make some tweaks so that it does all the things you want it to do (like giving people a way to contact you and providing some information about you and your products), but this is major progress!

    Congratulations!

If you want to pat yourself on the back and knock off for the day, that's perfectly fine!

In the next section, we will go through the basic setup and get you adding content.

This is one of the most technical sections thus far, so I am going to just stick a little FAQ section right here, in case you have one of these questions. Feel free to ask me more over at www.loriculwell.com!

Q: That seemed really complicated. Why are we doing this again?

    A: This is the part where I am trying to help you save money on monthly fees by doing the installation yourself. Since the Word-

Press installation is something you can learn and repeat, I figured it was a good opportunity to cut that line item out of your budget so you can use it for something else.

Q: That was awful, and I'm positive I'm never going to do it.

A: If you found this section absolutely horrifying (to the point where you know you will never do it), there is a solution! Go back to the chapter on hosting, find the "WordPress Hosting" section, and sign up for one of those accounts. HostGator is the best-priced and has the best tech support, but all of them would work for your purposes. Call up your hosting company and tell them you bought the wrong thing. Get them to refund your shared hosting and sell you some WordPress hosting. They will be only too happy to sell you a higher-priced product, trust me!

Q: My hosting company is not in your list of examples, and I can't find the cPanel.

A: Yeah, some of them are super hard to find, and I'm not sure why. This is when I would call your hosting company's tech support and have them walk you through exactly where it is, or Google "hosting company + cpanel" and read their help documentation.

Q: I made it to the end, but I never got the email with my installation details.

A: Check your spam filter!

Q: I don't think that installation worked. Is my website ruined?

A: Not at all! You can erase the whole installation and start all over. One of the best things about WordPress is that it is super flexible like that.

Q: Wait—did you just say my website was now "live"? What if people see it? Should I put it in "Under Construction" mode?

A: Don't panic! No one is going to see your website unless you tell them to go over and look at it, and it takes awhile for Google to notice your website even when you want it to. Your website is as good as invisible right now, I can assure you. I don't recommend "Under Construction" mode because I find that if I tell people how to turn that on, they sometimes leave it on and never finish their websites. I know, that's not going to be you, but leave it up! Knowing the search engines are going to come around in a few weeks will push you to work on the website!

9
THE BASIC SETUP

Whoa! Your website is live!

I don't want to scare you, but if you go over to yourdomain.com right now, your website is *actually on the internet.*

Well—that snuck up on us a little bit, didn't it?

Don't panic. It *is* live, but no one's going to see it yet, so don't worry. As I mentioned in the last section, Google's algorithm actually takes a little while to "notice" your website, and no one that you know personally is going to actually type in your web address to go and look at it until you give them the link, so you're fine to be building on it in its "live" state for a week or two.

. . .

The very first thing to do is go over to your website's backend, which can now be found at http://yourdomain.com/wp-admin (obviously, replace "yourdomain" with your actual domain). Grab the login credentials from your "Central Info" document (see how handy that thing is?) and make sure you can get in. Click the "Remember Me" box so it remembers you, because you're going to be going there multiple times a day from now on, right?

We're about to have a nice moment here (provided you took my advice back in Chapter 4 and did those writing exercises). Right now, pull out that writing you did right after you finished your keyword research (before you even bought your domain).

If you didn't do those exercises, that is also fine! There is still time! Go back and do them now.

Here is the back-end of your WordPress installation, which is where you will go to make all the changes to your website.

The very first thing we're going to do is go in and add some plugins, mostly for security and ease of use. Plugins are little pieces of code that make your site work better, and I have some that I like to install before I even start adding content to a site.

Go to "Plugins> Add New Plugin" in the sidebar.

That looks like this:

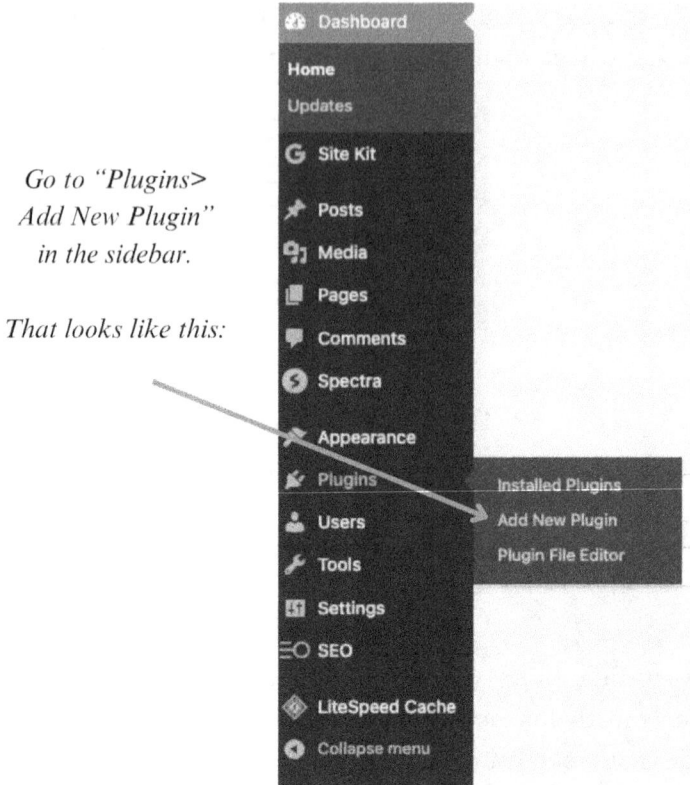

Install and activate the following plugins. Classic Editor is usually in the menu already, and you can find the others by searching in the search plugins on the top right.

—Wordfence Security
  —Classic Editor
  — SiteKit by Google
  — Redirection

. . .

One Quick Setting to Change

While we're still in "setup" mode, we'll do a couple of things that are good to get out of the way before you add content.

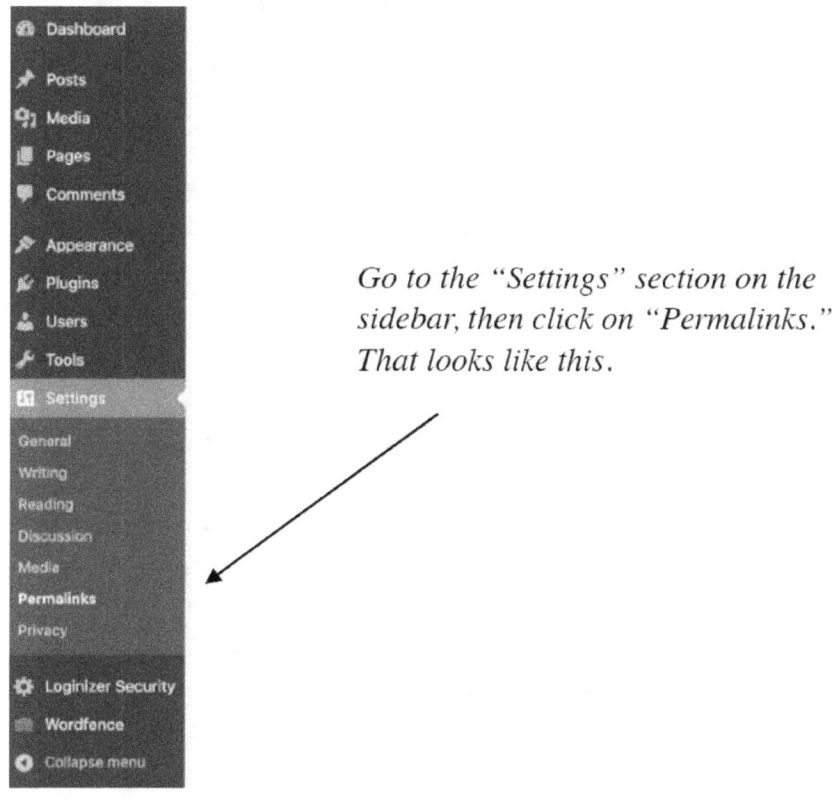

Go to the "Settings" section on the sidebar, then click on "Permalinks." That looks like this.

You want the "Post Name" setting, which looks like this:

⦿ Post name
   https://yourdomainname.com/sample-post

Save that setting and go back up to the main "Plugins" screen.

In case you're mentally cursing me right now and wondering why I am being so mean and forcing you to do this on your very first day with WordPress, the reason is this: these are the things that are going to really bite you in the ass if you wait too long to do them.

For example, if you set your whole site up but don't have a security plugin in place, you are going to be super pissed if you get hacked and have to rebuild the whole thing from scratch (or pay someone to recover it).

Wordfence solves that problem.

Another example: the default permalink setting for WordPress publishes your posts with the numbered dates in each and every URL. That is unsightly and bad for SEO, and what you don't want to do is realize this *after* you've already put up 100 blog posts, which you will then have to go back and manually change one by one. Changing the permalink setting to "post name" solves that problem.

. . .

And so on. This is my fail-safe list of setup items that I compiled while setting up something like 1,000 WordPress installations over the years. As you get more familiar with WordPress, you are going to find the tweaks and changes that work for you.

Start Adding Content!

After you have those key plugins installed and activated, and you've changed the permalinks, click "Dashboard" in the upper left.

You'll want to jump right in and start adding things, mostly to get comfortable with the interface (and to recover from that last chapter). Click "Add New Post," which you can find in the sidebar under "Posts."

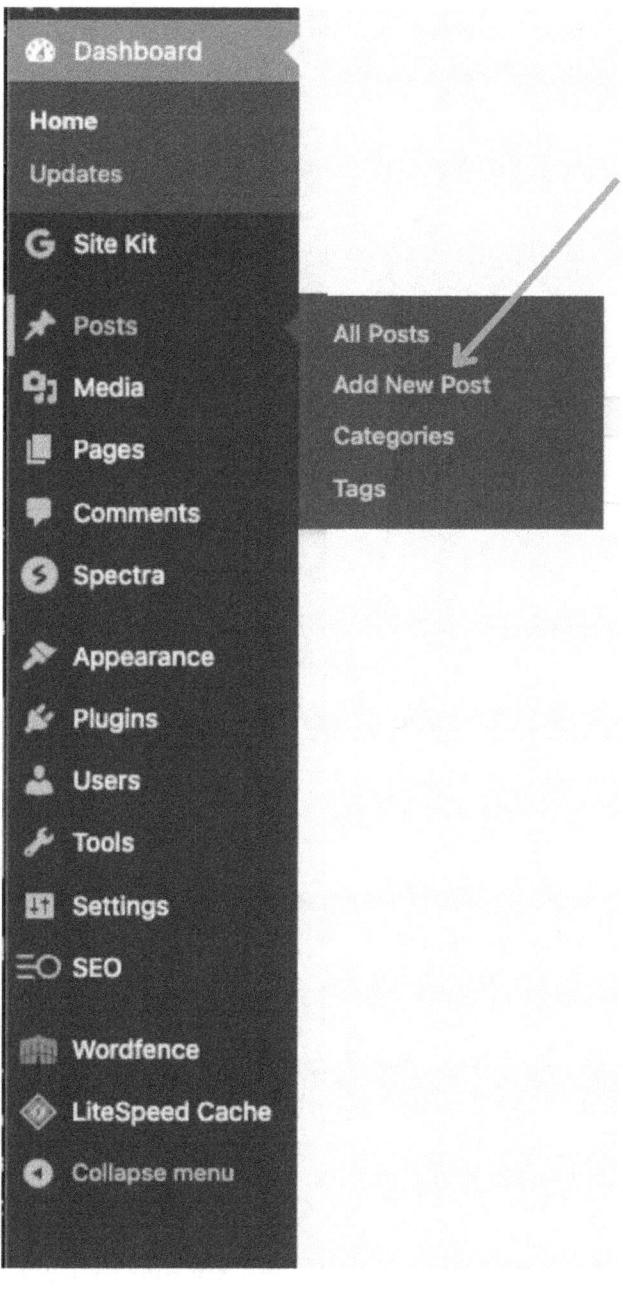

The "blank post" screen looks like this:

Okay, now go back to Chapter 4 and grab the "Welcome" blurb that you wrote.

Wait—what?!

If you still didn't do this, you are *so mad* right now! But... are you mad at me, or are you mad at yourself?

Go get it, or go back to Chapter 4 and do all of that writing. For real, this is when you need it!

Copy/paste your "Welcome" text into the body of this post, then hit "Publish." If you have any other pre-written posts (based on your keyword research), set those up as new posts as well.

Once you have populated the blog with a few pre-written posts, hit the "Dashboard" button, which will bring you back to the dashboard (imagine that!) Go back to the sidebar, go to Pages, and click "Add New Page."

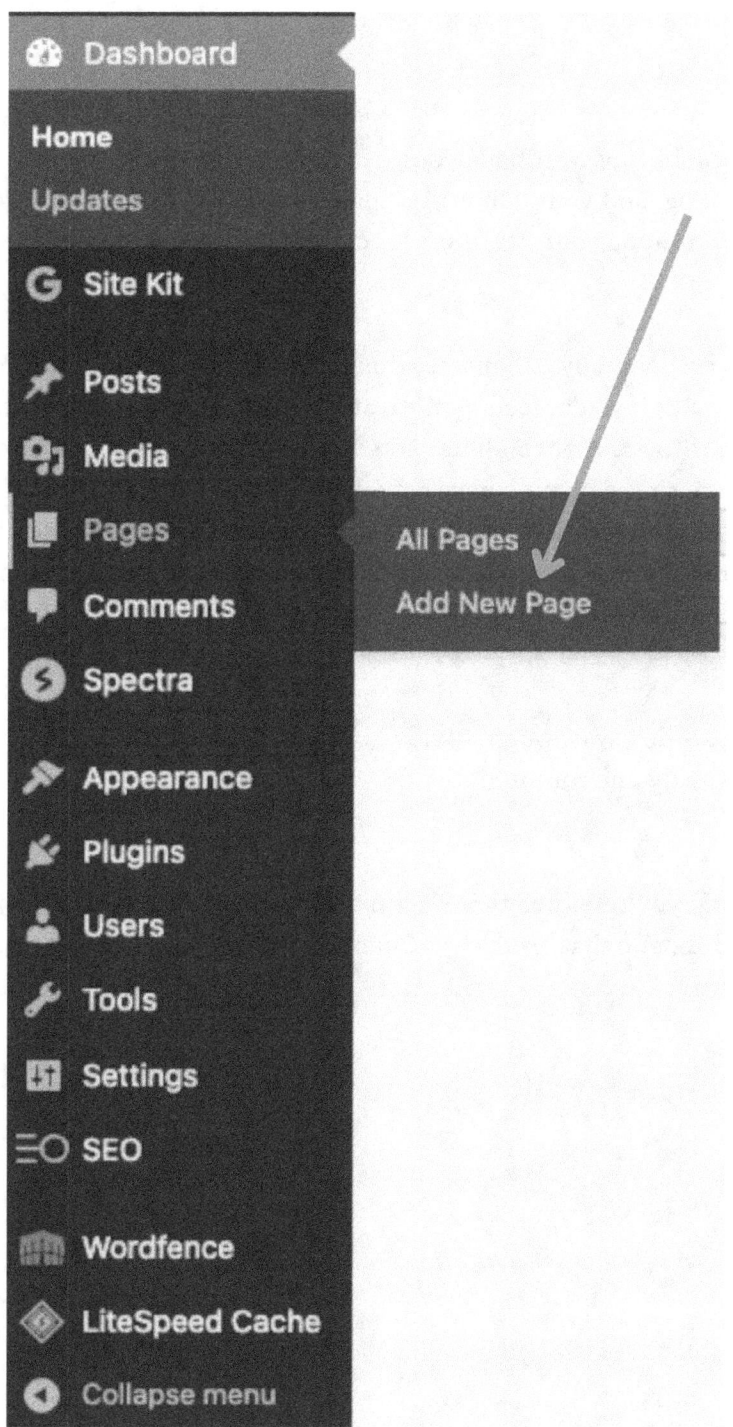

. . .

Great job! Now you have your basic setup done, you've launched your blog, and your "About Us" page is live. Now even if someone happens upon your site, there is actually something there!

If you're mentally exhausted, this would be a good time to take a break. But if you're feeling motivated, you're now welcome to click around the rest of the blue links in the "Welcome to WordPress" section, since you now have actual content on your site and will be able to see how the WordPress editor moves it around. Remember, the more you log in and make changes and additions, the more you'll get used to it.

That section was rough, I know, but you made it! You now have a website up and running!

(Again, you're either thanking me right now, or you're still mad you didn't do that exercise in Chapter 4.)

10

HOW WILL IT LOOK?

Now that you have some of the initial settings out of the way and you've got some content on your site (blog posts and the About Us page), you've probably started thinking about how you want the site to look.

Your initial reaction at this point might be: "I am not a designer, and I have no interest in this."

Believe me, I get it. I am also not a designer. Remember, you can quit this whole "theme" thing and hire someone to do this for you at any time. If you already want to do that, go right on over to Chapter 13! However, I think it's good for you to learn some of this stuff, just so you can make your site look decent while you wait for your official design to be done. SEO-wise, it's better to start putting content on your site and let it marinate in the search engines while you settle on the perfect design (rather than waiting to launch it until you think it is perfect).

. . .

Let's go over and take a look at your site. By now you have seen your homepage at least once (probably after you added the blog posts and About page). At first glance, you might have said "Whoa! I do not like that at all! I would like to erase this website and quit."

That is totally normal. No one likes their website when they first look at it. It's a process. This is actually a good moment to start talking about **themes**. The reason your website has birds on it right now is because the theme that appears by default when you install WordPress is "Twenty Twenty-Five."

Themes are different designs that you can apply to your site that will give it a different look (and sometimes different functions). The great thing about WordPress is that you can change the theme at any time, so you can keep switching it up until you find something you love.

. . .

Look around your site with the Twenty Twenty-Five theme installed. Make some notes about what you like and don't like. For example, if you are already thinking things like "I would like the author name and date to not appear under the post," or "I don't want the word 'Uncategorized' there," please get a notebook and start writing those things down. We will cover fine-tuning when we have this general theme concept out of the way. I mean, good looking out and all, but I really don't advise fixing stuff like that until you've decided on a theme, or you will fall down a YouTube tutorial rabbit hole and make yourself crazy.

Back to themes!

There are three ways you can go with your site design, and we'll talk about each one of them in its own chapter so you can confidently decide which way to go. Even if you're planning on hiring a designer to completely trick out your website (which is absolutely fine!), I would still recommend reading through these sections, just to familiarize yourself with the terminology and to give yourself a basis of understanding, so you know what to ask for when hiring a designer. The more you know, the more money you'll save!

Here are the three ways to get themes and designs, listed in order of cost:

Free: This is when you use one of the many, many (many!) free designs in the WordPress "Free Themes" marketplace/directory. These themes are all created by independent designers and developers, and are free for you to use as you see fit. I will cover the pros and cons of using a free theme in the next chapter.

· · ·

Paid: This is when you buy an out-of-the-box paid theme from a marketplace, or purchase a license for "theme development/theme builder" software that will allow you to create something more custom. Don't worry if you don't know what I'm talking about right now. We'll get there!

Custom/Designer: This is when you hire a designer to make a design for you (they might also call it a custom theme). I have no problem with people doing this, and in fact, I have some good friends that are designers! I just think that before you jump right in and hire someone, you should look over all of your options. If and when you do end up hiring a designer, you will both be glad that you took the time to learn a little bit and make some decisions about what you want.

That's it for my introduction to themes. Wasn't as terrible as you thought, right? Now let's go right over and start talking free themes while we have some momentum!

11
FREE THEMES

In this section, we're going to go over how to find free themes and let you try some out. If you find one that you end up loving, great! You're done and it was free. This guide just paid for itself, and my work here is done.

Kidding! Free themes are probably not going to fulfill all of your design and functionality needs, but you should know about them, at least at the beginning of your website setup journey.

The first thing you need to know is where to *find* the free themes. The marketplace can be accessed from right there in your dashboard, so go ahead and log in to the back-end of your site, at https://yourdomain.com/wp-admin

Look for "Appearance" in the sidebar, then click on "Themes." That looks like this:

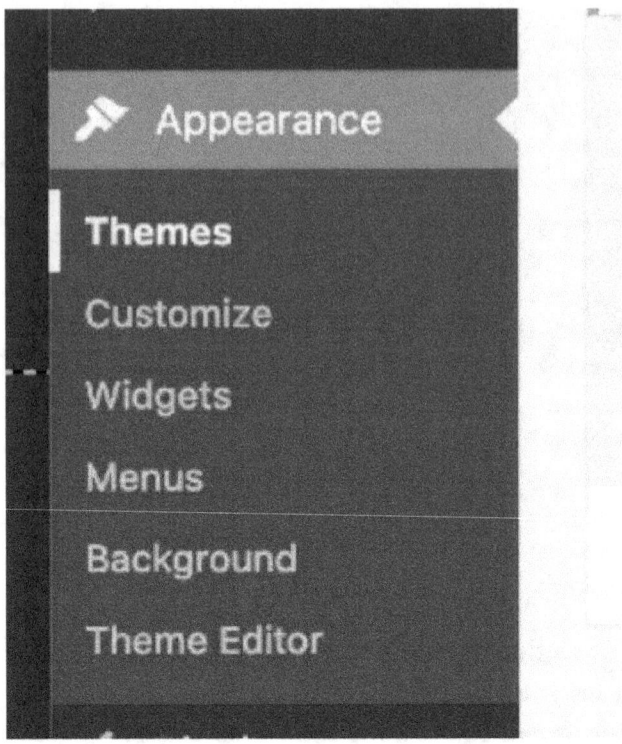

WordPress provides a few default theme choices with the initial installation, and that's what you see when you arrive at the "Themes" section.

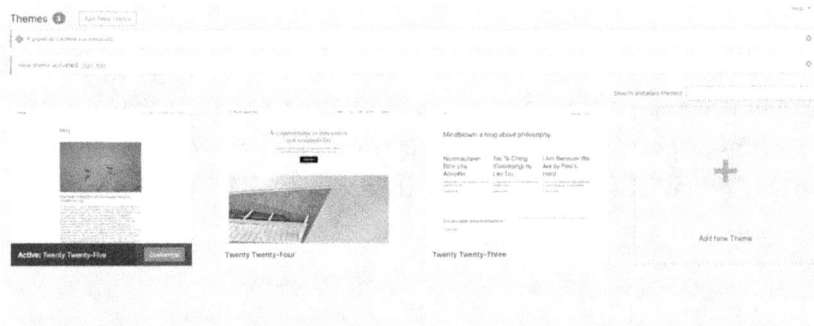

FUNNY YOU SHOULD ASK HOW TO MAKE A WEBSITE   115

. . .

What I would recommend you do right now is to go to the "Live Preview" button for each of these themes and take a look at how your website would look with that theme applied. It's a fun exercise and really gives you a feel for how much flexibility WordPress gives you.

When you're done with that, click the "Add New" button, which will take you to the marketplace and directory of free themes.

There are thousands (if not hundreds of thousands) of free themes in the marketplace, so brace yourself. The amount of choice might be overwhelming at first.

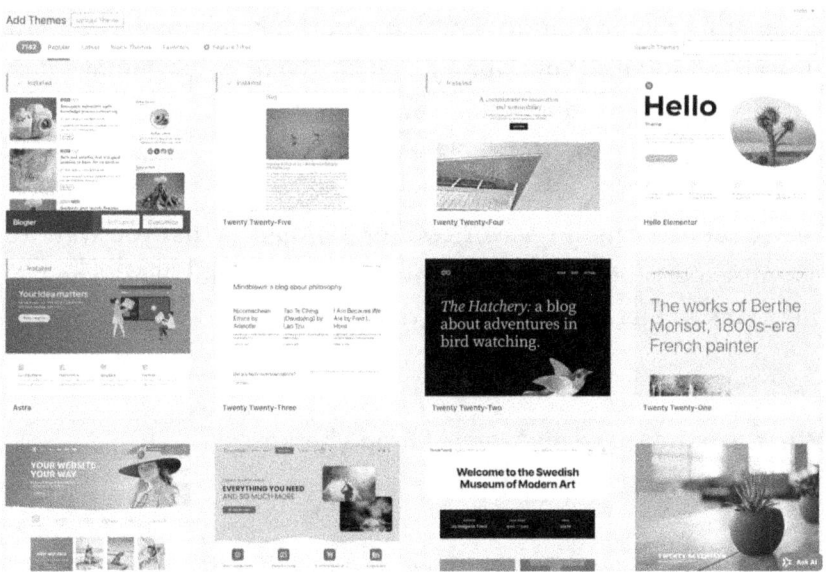

As you can see, there are a ton of good choices, and you're free to hit that "Preview" button on each and every one of them so you can see how your site would look with that design. The preview makes it so you don't even have to install it to see how it would look. Pretty cool, right?

Once you've exhausted the themes in the "Featured" screen, feel free to go over to "Popular, Latest, and Favorites."

Another option for finding themes is to use the "Search Themes" box, where you'll basically just put in keywords like "blog" or "store" or "publisher" (or whatever you think your site is going to be) until you find something that looks good and will work for your site's needs.

If something jumps out at you that you think you might love, hit "Install" to add it to your library, and "Activate" when you want to actually apply it to your site. Super simple!

You've probably found one or two (or 35) themes that you want to try out, so I will just quickly answer some standard "Free Theme" questions and let you get back to that.

What Are the Disadvantages of Free Themes?

Probably the biggest disadvantage you're going to encounter with a free theme is that when you want to customize something that isn't covered by the pre-made design (like moving the navigation around or making the header graphic bigger), you are going to have to figure out how to do it yourself. That process quickly becomes a "you got what you paid for" situation and can be frustrating. Free themes are usually made by designers and developers as "lead magnets" for paid themes, so there is no tech support unless you want to buy their paid option. Makes sense, right?

The free solution for this is to Google "Theme name + [what you're trying to do]." Chances are, someone has invented a plugin that solves the problem (and we will cover plugins when we're done with themes), or someone had the same problem, solved it, and made a YouTube video or a blog post about it. WordPress is all open source, allowing people to come up with clever solutions and share them with each other.

The paid solution for this is to get your site as far as you can get it with the free theme, then hire a designer/developer to just come in for a few hours and make a list of tweaks at the very end. That way, you did most of the work yourself and are just paying someone to do the things you absolutely cannot figure out, rather than paying thousands of dollars for a design—and the implementation of that design.

I always encourage anyone with a brand-new website to just go through the process of picking a free theme, installing it, and playing around with it. Doing this will give you confidence (you can switch your theme without crashing your site!), plus it will give you some ideas of what you want your site to look like. Even if you don't end up sticking with the free theme, there is value in looking at your content through some different lenses so you can further refine your vision.

. . .

Once you've settled on a couple of themes you think you might try out, I would recommend going through and deleting the rest of the themes you installed during this process. I say this because there is no need to have a bunch of random code (in the form of themes you're not using) sitting on the back end of your site. Extra themes take up space on your hosting account and sometimes cause conflicts with one another if they don't get updated regularly, so I would recommend getting rid of anything you're not using, just to keep things clean and streamlined. If you want to keep them for whatever reason, just be sure to go in and enable the auto-update function for each and every theme, so you don't have to do that manually every time a new update is released.

Now that you're familiar with free themes, let's move on to paid themes and theme-building software, which will give you many more options for the design and functionality of your site!

12

PAID THEMES/ THEME BUILDERS

OK, you've taken a look at the "free themes" marketplace and have hopefully tried out one or more of those themes on your website. This might be good enough for now, and if it is, great, you can skip this section until your site has a chance to grow a little bit. However, be sure to come back and read it before you buy a paid theme (or theme builder) or hire a designer.

At a certain point (either now or when your website has grown), you might decide that you want something even fancier with more features, and that's going to mean buying a paid theme or a theme/website builder.

What's the difference? A *paid theme* is a design with one fixed theme, whereas a *theme/website builder* has multiple preset themes to choose from and more functionality for building and customizing your site. A paid theme is going to cost a little less than a whole theme-building system, which you probably could have guessed.

Here's an example for Steve the Sourdough Guy (no, I am never going to let this example go):

When Steve decides he wants his website to look better and do more than the free theme he initially chose, he can spring for a food-related theme.

Here's a lovely one he might like:

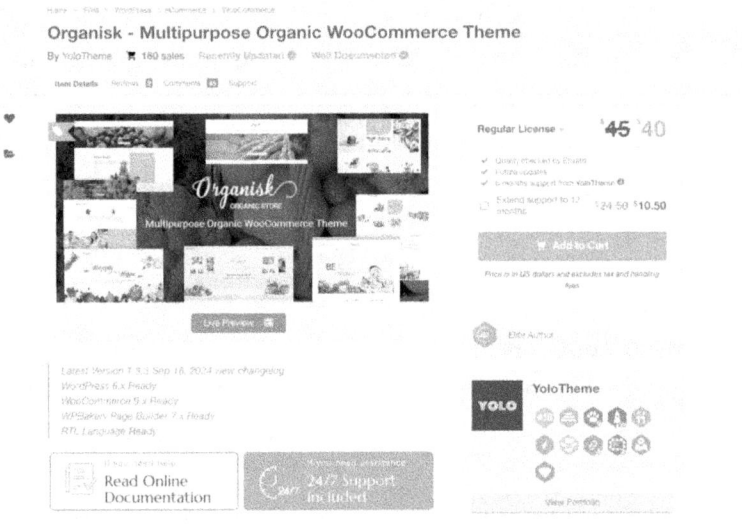

For the purposes of this never-ending example, Steve would pay the $40 for this theme, install it, and then adjust it until it looks the way he wants it.

However, if Steve already knows he's going to want something fancier and more functional than a free theme but wants even more flexibility than a single paid theme, he would go ahead and pay a little more for a website builder.

Some examples of builders include Avada:

https://themeforest.net/item/avada-responsive-multipurpose-theme/2833226

Divi:

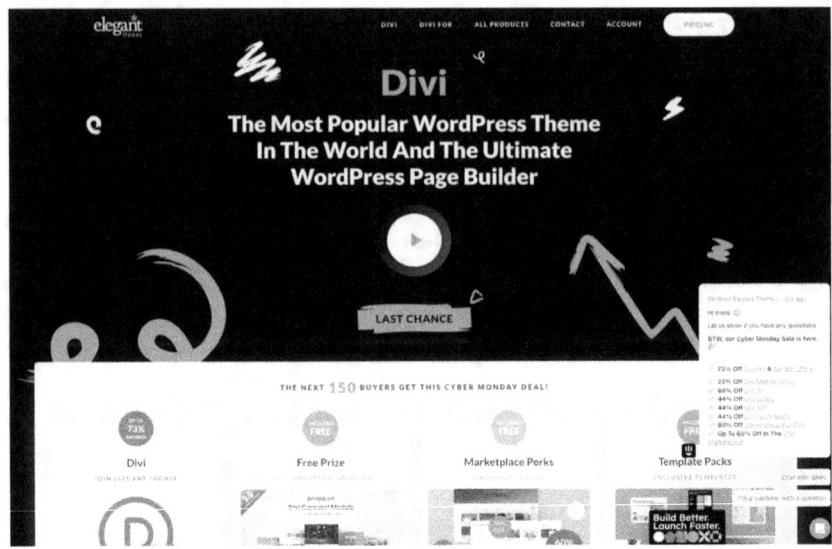

https://www.elegantthemes.com/gallery/divi/

and Elementor:

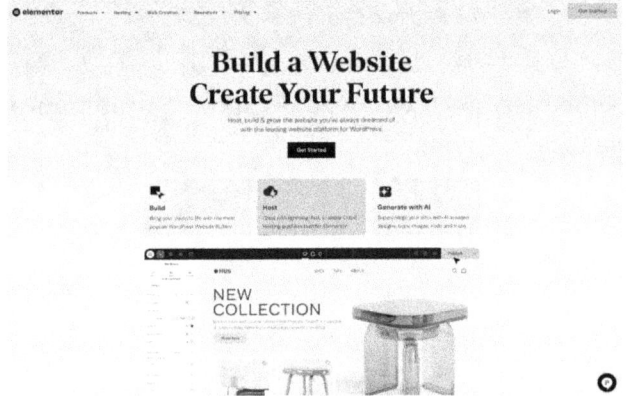

https://elementor.com/

. . .

Obviously, Steve (and you!) would have to visit each site, compare the pricing, look at the presets, and figure out which system sounds like it's going to work the best for the project. One important thing to remember is that every single theme (free or paid) or theme builder is going to require some tweaking to get your site exactly the way you want it. Do not fall into the trap of thinking that just because you paid for a theme, it's going to come out of the box looking great. Getting your site the way you want it is going to take some work no matter what!

Believe it or not, for once I do not have a generic recommendation for best paid theme or best theme/website builder. I have seen many different paid themes and builders work great for different projects, so I don't want to limit your research process by recommending something that might not end up working for your needs.

I've compiled a list of places to find themes/theme builders at the end of this section, so skip to that part if you want to take some time to browse around and decide! If you've already picked something, here are some one-size-fits-all installation instructions to help you get started.

Installation instructions

When you buy a paid theme/theme builder, the developer (or company) will send you a download link and (hopefully) some installation instructions in an email. This is going to look a little different depending on which theme you buy, but is pretty much always going to involve you downloading a zip file of the theme and then uploading it into the backend of your WordPress installation.

Right now you're like, "Huh? I'm just trying to make my website look good. I am not trying to be a website developer."

I get it. Hang in there. The instructions might be a little confusing, but you're almost there. The bottom line is: download the *zip file* of the new theme and pull that over to your desktop (or wherever you put downloaded things that you want to be able to easily find again).

Once you've saved that zip file somewhere findable, head over to Appearance> Themes (just like in the "Free Themes" section).

If you didn't read that section or you've already put that information out of your mind, that's okay! You're looking for this:

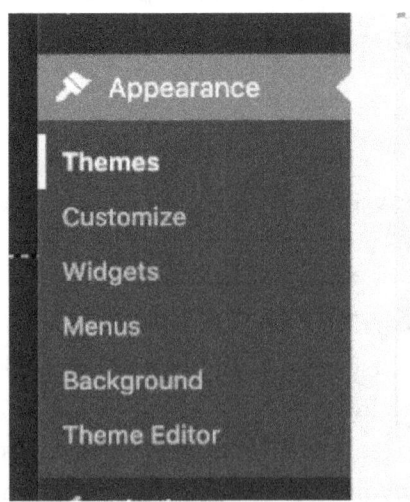

Just like in the "Free Themes" section, you'll click the "Add New" button at the top of the "Themes" screen, only this time you'll take it one step further and click the "Upload Theme" button.

This is when you're going to be super happy you put that zip file in a findable place, because without warning, this scary screen appears:

If you have a theme in a .zip format, you may install or update it by uploading it here.

Choose File | No file chosen   Install Now

You're prepared, though, so you won't panic. Click "Choose File," locate the zip file, and click "Install Now." That theme will then be available in your theme library, and you can go and activate it.

Once your theme is installed, the best way to avoid complete overwhelm is to start toggling back and forth between the front-end of your site (yourdomain.com) and the back-end (yourdomain.com/wp-admin) and moving things around until the site starts to look the way you want it. It helps to have specific goals in mind, like "I am trying to put my logo on the homepage," or "I would like to collect people's email addresses," because then you can learn the functionality as you go without disappearing down a rabbit hole of frustration and angst. Having something you're actually trying to do is always better than just staring at a bunch of new technology and trying to learn it "because you should." When has that ever worked? No, what you're trying to do here is use the technology to get your website to actually start looking and behaving the way you see it in your mind. Start from the end, and you will be more likely to push through!

As I mentioned, this is not going to be an out-of-the-box situation and is going to take some tweaking (depending on the look you're trying to achieve for the site) plus a lot of patience. The good thing about paid themes/theme builders is that they usually come with a lot of documentation and tutorials, and there's also usually the option to buy additional tech support and design help if you need it.

Most themes also have a money-back guarantee, so if you buy one and absolutely hate it, you can get your money back. This is something you should look for while you're searching around, just in case.

My suggestion for this is to not try to do all of this in one day. This is going to be an iterative process, and you'll need to be prepared for a learning curve, some frustration, and some swearing. We've all been there! You can also do the thing that I recommended with the free themes, which is to get your site as far as you can on your own (while keeping a list of things you can"t figure out as you go), and then hire a designer to come in and do the rest for you.

Great job! This is a lot to understand all at once, and if you've made it this far, you are well on your way to having your perfect website!

At this point I would recommend going to Chapter 14 because that is when we are going to start putting the content on your site. However, if you've gotten this far and you've now officially decided there is no way you're ever going to do any of these things, that's also fine! You gave it a chance, and the next section is all about finding and hiring a designer. :)

Here are some popular places to look for paid WordPress themes:
    Envato Market: http://themeforest.net
    Creative Market: http://creativemarket.com

Here is a list of popular theme builders:
    https://www.designbombs.com/best-drag-and-drop-theme-builders-for-wordpress/

I will also list the ones I have heard of here in case you want to just click over and start checking them out:

Avada

https://themeforest.net/item/avada-responsive-multipurpose-theme/2833226

Beaver Builder: https://www.wpbeaverbuilder.com/

Divi: https://www.elegantthemes.com/gallery/divi/

Elementor: https://elementor.com/

Themify: https://themify.me/builder

Thrive Theme Builder: https://thrivethemes.com/themebuilder/

13
FINE! HIRE A DESIGNER!

If you've reviewed all of your options for themes and have officially decided that you'd rather spend the money on a designer or developer, great! It's good to make that decision (and spend that money) from an informed and confident place, rather than feeling like you are shelling out a bunch of money because you just don't know what else to do. I'm not trying to stop you!

Before we proceed, however, I will offer a word of caution. As you probably gathered from the first couple of sections, I am a huge believer that you should put everything in your own name from the beginning. I have seen this particular situation go off the rails more times than I can count, so I will open this section by once again reminding you that even if you're going to have a designer make (and even maintain) your site for you, you still want to have your domain, your hosting, and all of your accounts in your own name. You might be best friends with your designer/developer after this process is over, but you still want to be able to pay the bill and walk away with your property if anything goes wrong. Your designer should want that for you!

OK, rant over. Thanks for coming to my TED Talk.

Before you start looking around for designers, the first thing you'll need to do is spend some time thinking about how you want your site to look and what you're going to want it to do. By "spend some time," I mean actually write these things down! You don't have to put a whole design brief together, but you do need some idea of what you want, because if you approach a design process saying, "I don't know, do whatever *you* think is best," two things will happen: 1) you will end up overpaying, and 2) you and the designer will both end up frustrated.

Right now, before we go any further, take out some paper (or open up a file on your computer, or go and get that free printable guide I've been talking about) and start writing some stuff down. In fact, answer these questions! You are going to end up answering them anyway once you find a designer, and I promise you it is cheaper for you to sit and answer them right now, as opposed to waiting until you sign a contract and then paying the designer to pull these answers out of you (or worse, paying for a design that ends up being a like a first draft because you didn't refine your vision before you started the process).

Ten Questions to Answer Before You Hire a Designer
Purpose & Functionality

1. What is the purpose of your website?
2. What do you want the site to do?
3. No, really. What do you want it to *do*? Do you want to be able to sell stuff (i.e. collect money) on this website? What about email signup? Are you featuring your writing in the form of a blog? Do you want to showcase some videos? What about social media accounts? Right now, do a brain dump of all the things you might want your website to do, now and in the future. Leave no stone unturned. I'm serious.

Look & Feel

4. What are some comparable sites that do the same thing you want yours to do? Write down 5-10 entities that you see as competitors—even if those competitors take the form of major brands.

5. Of those, which ones do you like? Spend some time actually looking at them, and then write down the things you like. Do you

like the color combinations? Are you impressed with a certain piece of functionality? Write that down!

6. Do you have a color palette or a look and feel in mind based on the niche or genre of your site? For example, have you noticed that all other organic bread bakers have clean white sites? Do you want to go *with* this trend? *Against* it? Or do you want to meet somewhere in the middle? Make some notes about that!

Budget

7. What is your total budget for this site's design and implementation? Write this number down so that you know it, but *do not* tell it to the designer (at least not initially). This is just for your reference, so you can compare it to the quote you get from the designer and negotiate accordingly.

8. If the design proposal ends up exceeding your budget, think about what you'd be willing to give up. Do you want a great-looking site that does a little less of your "wish list," or do you want functionality over aesthetics? Once your site takes off, you can go back and make improvements, but if you're trying to stay within a budget range, you'll need to decide what's important to you before you even start, so you can be decisive with the designer and keep the project moving.

Timing

9. What is your desired launch date? Are you going to wait until that date to start telling people about the site or sharing it on social media? Does this date work with the designer's schedule? Is

it going to cost more for them to bump another project? Talk about this up front.

Side note: I still think your site should be live and that you should be putting content on it (in the form of excellent blog posts) the whole time the designer is working on it. Remember, Google cares about words, not designs, so the more time your words have to marinate in the search engine, the better.

10. Are you absolutely sure you know every single thing you want right now? Every time you make a change that is outside the scope of the original contract, *you* are likely pushing the launch date back and increasing the cost. The designer may not say that to you right then, because they may assume you know this, so I am telling you!

Great! Now that you have all of that written down, you'll be in good shape to start looking around for a designer/developer.

You'll need someone who can work with a WordPress backend, and no, you will not consider switching your whole site over to html, or Wix, or Squarespace, or anything else. WordPress is what you're using, because it is easy to maintain it yourself, the search engines like it, and you've already installed it. Plus, this book is about WordPress, so that's what we're talking about. If you want to hear me ranting about how Wix and Squarespace throw off extraneous code at the expense of search engine rankings, go back to Chapter 1 because who doesn't enjoy a good rant?

Back to designers! You might already know someone who is a designer, or you may have found one just by asking around a little bit. If not, here are some suggestions for places you can look. The one thing I would *not* do is Google "website designer" and hire the first person who comes up, because what you're likely to get in that case is a designer whose strongest skill is actually SEO, and that is probably not going to go well.

Here are some places to find actual designers:

1. Ask your friends and colleagues. This is my first go-to method, and it usually works. If someone you know has a great-looking website, ask them who they used and whether they had a good experience.

2. Ask around locally. If you belong to a neighborhood or city group on Facebook or NextDoor, ask for names of local designers. Not only is it nice to support your community, but it can be easier to get through a website process if you're in the same time zone and can have some in-person meetings. Also, by doing this, you're likely to end up with some references from actual people rather than possibly fictional people on websites.

3. Try Upwork. If my first two methods didn't yield any designers (and I would be shocked if that were the case), go over to www.upwork.com and start a job. Upwork is a marketplace where you can post a job and find people to work on your projects. Just sign up and post a job on the Talent Marketplace, and you'll start getting applicants. Do make sure they have examples of actual websites they have designed, as well as references from clients they've successfully worked with in the past.

. . .

When you find your designer, you'll need to make sure to do the following to protect yourself (and them):

1. Sign a contract. They will most likely provide this, but if they don't, make sure you get in writing what you'll be paying and when the site will be delivered.

2. Do not pay for the entire site up-front. This probably goes without saying, but I'm going to say it anyway: agree on a deposit (no more than 50%), with the remainder due upon delivery.

3. Pay with a credit card or PayPal. These options offer you the most protection as a buyer, especially since you are technically buying something "electronic" that can't be held in your hands. Website design and development is a service, but you are buying the finished product, which is digital.

And with that, let's go back to adding content to your website. Even if you hire a designer, you are still going to have to do this because who is the expert in your subject matter, you or the designer? (Spoiler alert: It's you.)

Okay, then! Let's go learn some stuff about content strategy and plugins.

14
ADD CONTENT & PLUGINS

Believe it or not, we are, like, 75% done with this process right now. Since you're going to be constantly adding to and tweaking your site, getting the content basics (and the plugins to support them) out of the way is the next-to-last step.

Really! I am not even kidding! I know it feels like this setup process has taken forever, but we're almost to the part where you can just go and share your knowledge in the form of blog posts, thereby attracting millions of visitors to your site.

Now that you've decided on a design direction (by picking a free theme, buying a paid theme or theme builder, or hiring a designer), you'll need to make some decisions about your content and start adding stuff to the site. This is also where we're going to start talking about plugins. As I mentioned in the section on paid themes, it's better to try to learn this stuff from the perspective of something practical that you are trying to do, rather than approaching it from a purely "this is something I should know" standpoint. That never works!

So, what is "content?" You're probably aware, but all the words, photos, pages, blog posts, and little pieces of functionality (like the Contact Us form and links to social media) on a website are called the "content." Before you go putting this kind of stuff randomly onto your site, it helps to stop and consider your overall goals. The art (and science) of deciding what goes on your website is the "content strategy."

Right now, answer all of the following questions (and if you're feeling super motivated, turn them into a list). Like I said, it's easier to start with some goals in mind of what you want people to do on your site, then reverse-engineer the technology from there.

And no, you're not imagining things—this is a little bit of a repeat from the last section, but I figured not everyone was going to read that section, so I put it in here as well. I'm sneaky like that!

1. What is the overall purpose of your website?

This can be anything from "I want to sell sourdough bread," to "I want to give people the address and phone number of my dermatology practice and provide them with a list of services I offer." It's just super helpful to know from the beginning what you're trying to do with your website.

2. What do you want the site to do?

Right after you identify what the purpose of your website is, you'll want to start thinking about how the things you put on your site can help you accomplish those goals. Do you want to be able to sell stuff? What about collecting people's emails? Are you featuring your writing in the form of a blog? Do you want to showcase some videos? What about social media accounts? Right now, do a "brain dump" of all the things you might want your website to do (in pursuit of your overall goals), both now and in the future. Leave no stone unturned.

3. What will success look like to you?

Do you want to be number-one in Google for a specific search term? If so, why? What do you want people to do when they get to your site by Googling that term? Are you trying to sell people something related to that term (like a book on sourdough bread)? Whatever your goals, you'll need to set up some form of measurement or metrics so you can tell when you're achieving them! You'd be really surprised at how many people try to go with the "I'll know it when I see it" form of success measurement, then get upset when "it" never quite materializes.

In case you're afraid I'm going to leave you alone right now to reverse-engineer your whole list, do not worry! I'm obviously not there with you, so I can't provide an explanation for every specific thing you're trying to do on your site, but I am going to go through a couple of examples that will show you how to add some things that belong on all sites. From there, you'll be on the way to handling your list on your own. I believe in you!

Some of these things might theoretically be accomplished by the theme you've chosen (free, paid, theme-building situation, or designer), but since I don't know which one of those you went with, I have to assume that we're working with a bare-bones, free, limited functionality theme, so I'll walk you through how to get plugins to make your site do what you want it to do.

The "Contact Us" Page

Let's start with setting up the "Contact Us" page, which is something all sites need.

Google likes to see these pages on websites, and even if you want people to contact you solely through your social media, you'll still need a "Contact Us" page to point people to your socials (and to collect people's email addresses for your mailing list, if that's one of your goals). This part of your content strategy is to make it easy for people to contact you.

You already made your "About Us" page (right?), so you're familiar with how to make a page and write some stuff on it. If not, here's a little refresher.

Go to the "Pages" section of the sidebar and click "Add New."

Title the page "Contact Us," and write some catchy stuff on there about your mission for the site and about how you'd love to hear from people. You can feel free to repurpose the lovely prose you wrote for your "About Us" page, if you would like. Then, hit "Publish."

The next step is to go over to the Plugins section and get a contact form plugin. You can find several good ones by typing "contact" into the search bar in the plugin marketplace. Contact Form 7 is my personal go-to, but the form generator that comes with Jetpack is also good (and there are many others).

You'll want to use a contact form rather than just listing your email right there on your website, because email addresses on the internet get an alarming amount of spam.

Activate the contact form plugin, then go back over to your Contact Us page and set it up. They even provide you with instructions on how to do this!

Voila! You're done. You added the Contact Us page to your site. Now you're, like, 80% done with the setup.

Social Media Icons/Links on Homepage

Speaking of functionality, for our next example, let's look for a plugin to add some social media links to your homepage. As will quickly become a habit for you, when you need your website to do something, you'll turn once again to the plugin marketplace. Start typing in keywords like "social" and "homepage" until you hit upon something that sounds like what you need.

"Social Media Share" looks promising, so let's install it, activate it, and give it a shot. If it doesn't do what you want, you can always erase it and try another one (are you sensing a theme here?).

Email Sign-up

The next thing we'll work on is an email collection plugin because one thing I want almost everyone to do is start building their email lists. I could go on and on about this (and I do just that in other books), but for now, suffice it to say that I believe every website owner needs to be collecting the emails of anyone who is interested in their business. If you're already on top of this and you've signed up with an autoresponder service like MailerLite, AWeber, or GetResponse, you may already know that they provide plugins (which you can find in the marketplace) that will help with this. If not, I recommend going with a plugin like Hustle, which will walk you through some different methods of capturing emails (like pop-ups).

The bottom line is: when building out your site's functionality with plugins, it's helpful to think about what you're actually trying to do, then go look for the plugin (by using a keyword to search the marketplace). From there, install the plugin, activate it, and see if it does what you want. If it doesn't, deactivate and delete it, and try again!

Search Engine Optimization

This part of your content strategy is: "I would like the search engines to show my website to people who are searching for my topic, so those people can eventually become my customers."

SEO (Search Engine Optimization) is anything you do to your site so that search engines can more easily find it, consider it relevant, and show it to people who are searching. Plugins help with this by encouraging you to fill in SEO-friendly fields like keywords, title tags, and categories. My favorite plugin for SEO purposes is currently "All in One SEO" because it gives you an SEO score (for the page or post you're working on) as you go, but others seem to prefer the user interface of Yoast, which is also fine. Your theme might also have some built-in SEO features. If it does, use those rather than installing plugins. Do not use more than one SEO tool! There is such a thing as too much SEO! Google calls it "keyword stuffing" and will penalize you if they see you doing it. Pick one and go with it!

By the way, that is (by far) not all I have to say about SEO, but you need to put a plugin in place now to optimize your future SEO writing efforts. Trust me!

. . .

Statistics Measurement

In order to set some goals and grow your site, you'll eventually need to know how many visitors you're getting and how they're finding you. This is accomplished with a statistics plugin. If you're into Google Analytics, you'll enable that in your Google account, then install the Google SiteKit plugin, which will then prompt you to copy and paste the code. Easy peasy!

If you're not a Google Analytics fan (which is fine), some other options include Jetpack, Monster Insights, and WP-Stats. You can try any of them to see if they give you the data you want. The only one I'm not nuts about is Statpress Visitor because I don't think it tells you enough actionable stuff. You might love it though!

Even More Examples

Now that I have walked you through examples of both content and plugins that need to be on every site, I will cover some of the other things I think your website might need to do, with plugin recommendations for each. If you don't think you need your website to do any of these things, feel free to disregard! And, again, if you don't like a plugin I mention, try another one! This is an open-source world, my friends! It's a functionality free for all!

(Yes, I will stop with the exclamation points. I'm just excited about plugins, you guys. As a person who used to spend hours hand-coding html to make a website do even the most insignificant little thing, I think plugins are super neat.)

. . .

Disabling Comments. I would use this one to turn off comments on pages initially—and if you don't love having comments on your blog posts, I'd turn comments off there as well. This is one of those settings that can theoretically be done just in the back-end of WordPress, but for some reason, I find it works better when done with a plugin. If you don't care about comments in general, you can skip this one, although once you see the amount of comment spam that starts coming in when your site gets indexed by Google, you might change your mind. The plugins I use are "Disable Comments" and "Remove Comments & Stop Spam."

Removing Dates. It's possible that this is a thing that only bugs me, which is why it's way down in this section. I like my websites to have an evergreen quality, and I find that removing the dates from the posts on the blog accomplishes that. If you've had the experience where you're Googling around, find the answer to the question you're wondering about, then second-guess that answer because you notice it's on a blog post dated sometime in 2005, you can understand the importance of this feature. I have had good luck with the WP Meta and Date Remover plugin, and I have also tried Hide My Dates and WP Date Remover.

Plugin Best Practices

Before we leave this chapter, I will give you some of my best practices for plugins. I'm sure you're pretty burnt out by now, so I've crafted this into the form of a kicky Do's-and-Don'ts list.

. . .

DO: Look for a plugin that is up to date and tested with your version of WordPress.

Basically, you're looking for this:

Last Updated: 2 weeks ago

✓ **Compatible** with your version of WordPress

And you're trying to avoid this:

Last Updated: 2 months ago

Untested with your version of WordPress

The reason is simple: you do not want old code sitting on your website. If the developer doesn't believe in this plugin enough to keep it updated and compatible with the latest version of WordPress, chances are pretty good you're looking at a code conflict if you try to keep using that plugin. Lack of updates indicates the developer has pretty much abandoned that project, so they are not going to be available to help you out if that old code crashes your site.

DO: Set all of your plugins to "Enable Auto Updates."

. . .

When you have finalized all of the plugins you're going to use and have your site exactly the way you want it, I would recommend going into the main "Plugins" section and clicking "enable auto updates" on every plugin. That way, the plugins will update themselves and you won't have to think about them or worry about them aging and causing a conflict (which might crash your site). This will also keep you from having to manually make updates every time you log in to your site.

DO: Delete plugins you know you're not going to use.

During the trial-and-error and setup process, you will most likely install some plugins that will not end up being what you need.

When you've finalized your list of plugins and have your site exactly the way you want it, go back through and delete all of the rejects so that you have a streamlined list of plugins.

There is no need to have code sitting on your site that you're never going to use. Extraneous plugins take up space on your hosting account and sometimes cause conflicts with one another if they need updates. Troubleshooting a million unused plugins is going to take time and attention away from your goal of growing your website, so I would recommend going through and getting rid of anything you're not using, just to keep things clean and streamlined.

DO: Keep your eye out for new plugins.

. . .

If someone you know has a great-looking website, or if you happen upon a random website that does something you wish your website could do, look at the source code to play "plugin detective." Not only will this make you feel super smart, but your website will benefit!

Here is an example of how easy it is to look at another website's source code. Go over to the website, www.selfpublishingchecklist.com, then go to View> Developer> View Source in your Chrome browser (which looks like this):

You'll then see the source code for my website, which looks like this:

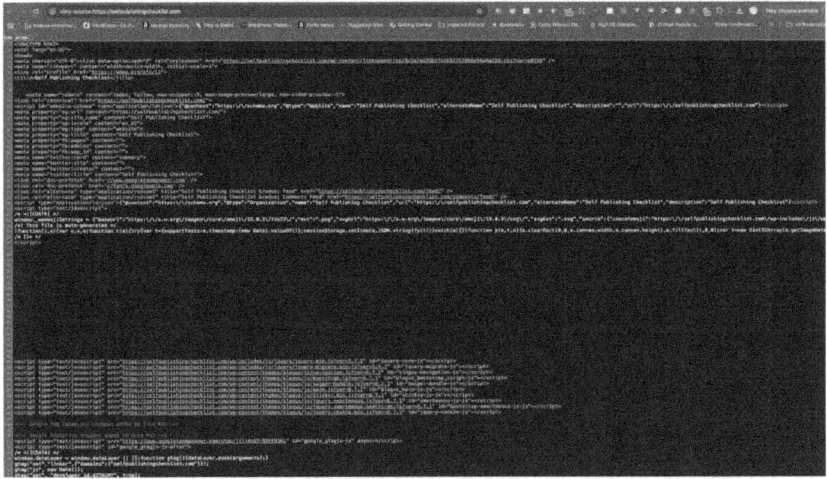

Don't even let the code intimidate you, because your WordPress installation is actually writing that for you. What you're looking for is the word "plugin," so you can see the list of plugins on the site. You can even do a "Control F" to find the word "plugin" if that's easier!

Write down the different plugins on the site, then go back over to the plugin marketplace in your own WordPress back-end to add them in. Occasionally you'll see someone using a premium (meaning paid) plugin, and you won't find that in the free marketplace. Usually, paid plugins can be found on www.themeforest.net, or you can Google the name of the plugin to find the developer and buy it from them.

The bottom line is—always be improving your website! If you see something that looks great on someone else's site, try it out!

That's it for the setup. In the next section we are going to cover my favorite subjects: SEO and writing!

15
THE BIG REVEAL!

Okay! Now that we have the main (and super tedious) setup done, we will move on to the meat-and-potatoes part of your website, which is your blog.

I'm really, really glad you've hung in there up to this point because this is when things get super exciting (and stay that way!). This strategy I am about to describe is by far the most effective way to get your website ranked for multiple search terms in Google, something that will get you free traffic, which in turn will get you customers (or sales, or whatever you're trying to do with your site).

How do I know this?

I don't want to toot my own horn here, but I'm afraid I'm going to have to because this is the exact strategy I used to rank a Fortune

100 website for over 35,000 keywords. If you're wondering how much you would have to pay for the kind of traffic that comes with that many organic rankings, I will tell you!

The answer is: half a million dollars per month.

$500,000 a month, people.

What I'm saying is this—you started a website because you're an expert, and right here is where you're going to start using your expertise to grow that sweet, sweet organic SEO traffic to your website so you will not have to pay to get people to go there. Because you took the time to set your site up properly, you are now going to swoop in and start doing blog posts like the rockstar you are, and Google is going to eat those posts up and reward you with rankings.

This, my friends, is where you are going to make your brand-new website invaluable to Google because you are going to become the source for the answers to all the questions everyone is asking about your chosen subject. Once Google realizes you are answering these questions, they are going to put you on Page One, not only for those questions and answers but for many of your other keyword terms as well.

Why didn't I tell you about this amazing strategy at the beginning of this guide? I do have a reason! I have found it to be universally true that once people hear about how powerful (and relatively easy) this strategy is, they want to start it right away, and so they skip the part where they actually set their website up properly. This leads to nightmare scenarios, like websites that are fantastically ranked but have no "Contact Us" page, no email sign-up, and no links to social media, so all of those leads (represented by the organic traffic) are falling through the cracks like the lost money that they are. *Yikes.*

I don't want that to happen to you, so I literally saved the best for last. Also, if you're reading this section and have done all the steps to set up your website properly, you are a winner, and I prefer to only share this killer strategy with winners. Yay!

Here's what we're going to do—pull out that keyword research you conducted way back in Chapter 3 using the software I recommended (Keyword Finder). Even if you didn't end up subscribing to the paid version (so you won't have it saved it there), you will still have the Excel spreadsheets you downloaded while you were doing that initial research. If you didn't do that step, do it right now!

Go ahead and call up one of those spreadsheets now. This is a list of keywords and key phrases that people are typing into Google about your chosen subject in numbers that are decent but that are not so competitive that you couldn't get your foot in the door with them, ranking-wise. In the sourdough bread example, we saw that there were several pockets of high interest and low competition around the terms "sourdough french bread" and "sourdough bread machine." I actually encouraged someone (anyone!) to start a website where you could not only offer sourdough bread recipes (and experiments), but you could also do reviews of things like sourdough bread makers and all other things sourdough.

. . .

(Seriously, if you start that sourdough site, let me know! I will send you all the research I have done for this example.)

Once you have located your sourdough-specific keyword lists, your next move is to go over to this website: http://answerthepublic.com. This is an awesome site that will take your keywords and tell you all the questions people are asking about those words. This will answer the question, "What do I write about?" so thoroughly, you are going to be blown away.

Go to the homepage of Answer the Public, type in your first low competition (green) keyword, and change the country to your preferred country.

FUNNY YOU SHOULD ASK HOW TO MAKE A WEBSITE

Here's an example!

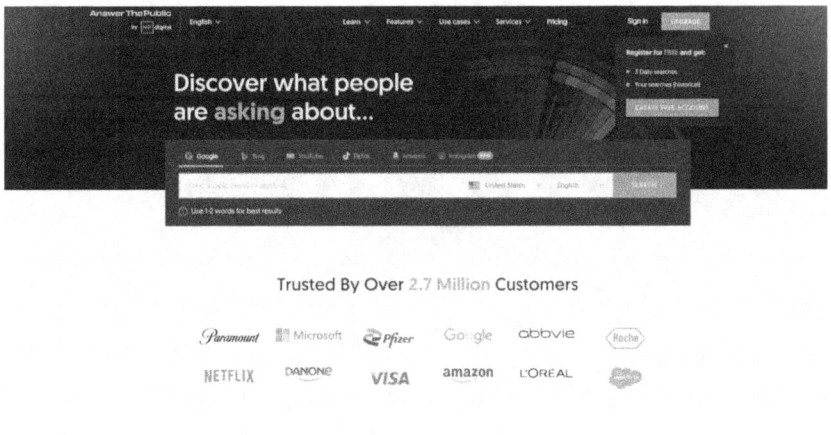

I put a little arrow there to remind you to please change the country (if you are in the United States). Answer the Public is a UK-based company, so it defaults to UK and British questions and spellings if you don't change it. (File that under Good to Know!)

Once you hit "search," Answer the Public's software will generate a killer list of actual questions and phrases that people are asking the internet about this topic. Here is what happened when I entered ONE search term: "sourdough french bread":

Whoa! SO many questions! Here are some real things people really want to know about the world of sourdough bread. As you can see, there are a bunch of great queries here, ranging from beginner ("What is sourdough french bread?") to more specific ("Is sourdough french bread low fodmap?").

This is where Answer the Public really knocks it out of the park and makes populating your blog with a great variety of terms super easy. Their method of research is hugely helpful for content creators because it shows you what people are actually asking in relation to your topic, so you never have to sit there with writer's block going "What should I write about?".

Just the phrase "sourdough french bread" yielded 75 questions (like the ones I mentioned above); 56 prepositions (like "sourdough french bread for diabetics") that you can easily make into questions, topics for posts, or jumping-off points for vlogs or social media posts; 15 comparisons (like "sourdough french bread vs. rye") that you can use as jumping-off points for posts; and 143 alphabeticals (sourdough french bread + a, b, and so on), so you know every single thing people want to know about that topic. That's a total of 222 blog post/content ideas for the phrase "sourdough french bread" alone.

Considering the fact that each keyword search on Keyword Finder gives you at least 25 additional keywords and phrases (each one of which you can then put into "Answer the Public" to generate another 350+ writing prompts), you now have a never-ending source of things to write about that will 100% get your site ranked, because these are real things that real people want to know about a topic in which you are an expert.

Um... that was kind of a big reveal, right? Your mind is probably reeling with all the possibilities right now, so I will quickly tell you how to execute this strategy and then let you get started setting everything up so that your genius can easily flow out in the form of optimized blog posts.

Once you decide on the first question you want to answer, open up the back-end of your website and click on Posts> Add New Post, which looks like this:

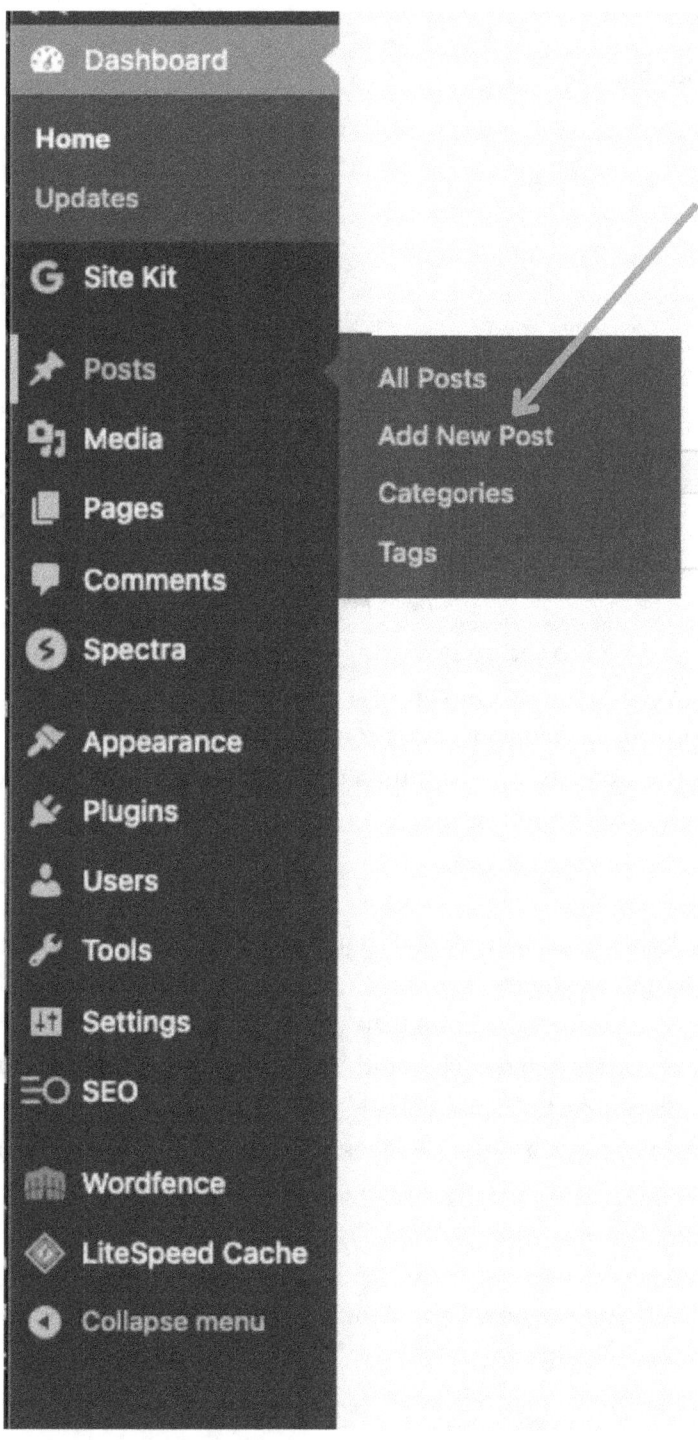

And this:

Take a question and put it in the "Add title" section.

Next, go down to the body of the post and use all of your expertise to answer that question the best way you can. Literally, pretend someone just asked you a question about this thing you know a lot about (because they pretty much did), and answer the question in as much detail as you can.

Please believe me when I say that there is no length of blog post that Google considers "too long." Google will be THRILLED if you want to go on for 2,000 or 3,000 words about the perfect moment to freeze sourdough french bread. And in fact, the longer you go on about this subject, the more likely you are to (unintentionally) do a thing that Google absolutely loves, a thing called "Latent Semantic Indexing."

Wow! Did you see how I snuck up on you with a nerdy SEO term? That was slick, right?

. . .

Latent semantic indexing, in case you are now totally curious (and I know you're not) is basically when you're talking about a topic and then start to use a lot of words *related* to that topic that only an expert would know. This kind of thing is what convinces Google that you are a super expert, and that's when they show you the SEO-love by ranking you for that term and many others.

Here's an example (not related to bread, because honestly, I don't know that much about bread):

Say you have a site about barbecuing. Amateur SEOs would go: "barbecues, barbecuing, BBQ, barbecue, barbecued, barbecue, barbecue grill, barbecue sauce, barbecue recipes," and so on. This kind of thing pisses off Google's algorithm because, hello, you're just repeating the same word over and over, and regular people don't talk like that.

Google's algorithm is smart, and it already knows all these duplicative and derivative terms. It knows that anyone who is searching for actual information on this subject is not going to be satisfied with a list like this, so it won't rank anything like this on Page One.

Pro SEOs invoke the magic of latent semantic indexing like this: "barbecue, grill, marinade, rub, spices, brush, tongs, fork, tongs, brush, skewers, baby back ribs."

And so on.

. . .

My point is—Google wants to see you using words that are related to your main topic because that's what shows them you're an expert. When you use this question-and-answer method, you set yourself up to slide right into the "LSI Zone," where you are going to automatically start talking about a bunch of different (but totally related) things.

Honestly, though, you don't even have to worry about knowing what latent semantic indexing is because you are going to be organically doing it when you answer all of these topic-related questions in your blog.

Believe it or not, we are almost at the very end of this guide. You now know not only how to set your website up but exactly what to write on it to get it found by the search engines. What else is there?

Really, just a couple of fine-tuning things I want to hit you with, plus some random stuff that I want you to know but that didn't really belong anywhere else. You're probably excited to start writing blog posts, so go with that energy right now!

16
NOW WHAT?!

Okay! You've set your website up. You've decided on a design (or a designer), and you're in the process of writing those 300+ topic-specific blog posts we talked about in the last section (the big reveal!)

You might be wondering—then what? Where do you go from here? You may not feel ready for me to just leave you to your own devices out there, but I'm here to tell you that if you made it through this whole guide and set up your website, you are actually kind of an expert now, and I am therefore about to start referring people who need websites over to you. Prepare yourself!

For real, though. Everything going forward is basically fine tuning, growth strategies, and occasional troubleshooting, so I have put together a list of questions that people usually ask me in the first six months after launching their website.

. . .

These are in no particular order and are not related to each other in terms of theme, so this section is maybe going to seem a little random. Feel free to just do a Ctrl F to look for topics if you don't want to read the whole thing in one sitting. I get it!

What should I be doing on an ongoing basis?

This is the first question that everyone asks when I hand them the "keys" to their brand-new website. I have two answers for this. The first answer is: use it! Write those blog posts from the last section and post one up every single day. Logging in every single day for the first month is the best way to learn the ins and outs of your website, to start coming up with ideas for new features you want or things you want to fine tune, and to generally get yourself over any lingering technological fear you might be having.

Log in every day! Make it a habit! Do not leave your site just sitting there gathering dust after you've put in all this work getting it up and running!

How can I tell if my site is "working"? How will I know what to change to make it better?

During the setup, I asked you to define what success looked like to you and to start installing measurement plugins accordingly. After your site has been live for about a month, you'll have some actual data to look at to determine what you should do next. Do you want to have 10,000 visitors per month? Do you want to get 100 new leads per month? Do you want to get 1,000,000 followers on social media?

Great! Record all of these stats on the first of every month and put them into a chart. Look at the data from the plugins (and add new plugins if you need to know even more!), run sales reports at the end of the month, record your social media numbers, and so on. Keep track of changes you make to the site, so you know when something makes a difference. When you find that thing (like a successful post), do more of that!

You can't grow what you don't measure, so keep a close eye on every stat that is important to you. If you sell things on your site, the main metric you'll want to work on is your conversion rate. You probably have an e-commerce plugin that tells you this (and if you don't, please get one).

Just to throw another fancy term at you, your **conversion rate** is defined as the number of visitors divided by the number of sales, meaning that if you have 1000 visitors to your website and 100 of them buy something, you have a 10% conversion rate. A "good" conversion rate is usually anything above 10%, so if you have that, you could set a goal to grow by 1% every month. Tweaking your content is one way of getting there. Try adjusting your product photos, sales copy, calls to action, or pricing. Get more reviews, and definitely fix anything customers have complained about. Basically, keep a close eye on your conversion rate and do what it takes to get it to improve.

If you want to know where your site is ranked for which keywords, I will refer you back to my favorite software, KeywordFinder, because they have a cool tracking feature. There's also a plugin for pretty much everything these days, so there's no reason not to know every single thing about your website that matters to your business.

My site crashed! Why? What should I do?

First of all, DO NOT PANIC when your site crashes. It's probably going to happen at some point. It happens to everyone! Yes, having your site be down is nerve-wracking, but it's not the end of the world—and you don't need to overpay to get it up and running again. Take a deep breath and go through this simple recovery checklist:

1. **Call the hosting company.** They might be able to tell you why the site is down. Maybe it's something they did! If the issue is on their end (like a server problem), they can fix it, or at least tell you when it's going to be fixed. This is when it's useful to have a hosting company with 24/7 tech support, because you can just call them to see if they know what is going on.

2. **Delete some old stuff.** If the problem isn't on the hosting side, the next most likely culprit will be a code conflict at the plugin or theme level. Since you will likely have "enable auto updates" turned on, it is possible that one of your plugins updated itself and caused a code conflict with something older, like a plugin or theme you're probably not using. These things happen! Try to stay calm. To see if this is the case, log in to the backend of your site via your hosting account's cPanel using the credentials you wrote down in your "Central Info" document. (Note: If you haven't logged in to your hosting in a long time or if you've forgotten how to do it, go back to Chapters 6 and 7, where I covered how to log in and where to look for your cPanel.) Each hosting account looks a little bit different, but here's basically what you'll do:

Control Panel

Email Accounts

Webmail

Databases

File Manager

Install WordPress

—Once you're in the cPanel, click "File Manager."

—Go all the way down to the "wp-content" folder and double click to expand it.

—Find the "plugins" folder and double click to expand it.

—Look at the "Last Modified" column to see if one of the plugins was updated in the past couple of days (or within the timeframe of the crash).

—Delete that plugin.

—Go back and check your website to see if it came back up.

—Repeat until your site comes back up.

Just to validate your feelings, yes, this is a super tedious process, and yes, you're going to end up having to reinstall those plugins (or find alternatives for them) once your site comes back up, but once you learn this process, it only takes a few minutes and can save you hundreds (possibly thousands) of dollars in tech fees and lost sales, so it's worth learning.

3. **Hire someone.** If you've tried Step 1 and Step 2 and your site has still not come back to life (or if you noticed any strange new activity on your site or in your plugins), there's a chance that, despite having Wordfence installed, your site has been hacked.

Again, remain calm. This is a thing that happens, and I have a solution. My favorite "hack fixer" is this guy on Fiverr: https://www.fiverr.com/sachinmaster

For $5, this guy will clean whatever nonsense has ended up on your site. You will need to provide him with the login details of your Wordpress installation and possibly the ftp info (again, look in your "Central Info" file).

Once he has fixed your site, be sure to change your passwords (which you should be doing on a regular basis anyway).

I super loved every single part of this guide! How can I get a job doing one or more of these things?

OK, I made the first part of that question up, but I actually have been asked the second part quite a bit, once people go through the process once and figure out that they like it.

. . .

Once you understand the process of setting up websites, you can absolutely make money doing it for other people. What you need is experience setting up a lot of websites so you can be fast enough to build up to a decent hourly rate, then you can specialize as you learn what you're really good at and what you like doing. I would recommend first setting up websites for your friends, family, and local businesses (either for free, trade, or for a discounted rate) to get some experience and references, and then when you're more confident, start a gig on Fiverr where you just set up people's WordPress installations for them. Once you get some good experience, you can branch out over to Upwork or start your own website!

I already had a website, but it was html-based. Anything I need to know before I transfer it over?

So, the good news is that you can do a lot of this yourself, which will be a relief, since html-based sites are usually developer dependent (even for updates). If you want to maintain the same look and feel of your current site, you'll need to hire a designer to do a WordPress conversion, taking your current design and converting it into a WordPress-friendly theme.

The most important things to remember when you are converting an existing site are: 1) be sure to back up absolutely all of your content before you start the process, and 2) once your site has been converted, make sure to use a plugin to redirect all of your old html-based links so you can keep all of the awesome links your previous site had.

I have a different keyword research tool that I like. Can I use that instead of the one you recommended?

Sure! Use whatever you like. I recommend Keyword Finder, because they color-code the low competition keywords, and I think that is super useful. I also like the rest of their tools, like the backlink finder and the ranking analysis, but if you don't want to use them, here's a list of other keyword tools you can totally use:

Google Keyword Planner http://ads.google.com
    SEM Rush http://www.semrush.com
    AHrefs http://www.ahrefs.com
    Moz: http://www.moz.com
    Keywords Everywhere: http://keywordseverywhere.com
    Ubersuggest: http://ubersuggest.io

That's it for my frequently asked questions, but let me know if there's anything else you'd like to hear about! I'm at www.loriculwell.com (and you can also find me all over social media). I would love to hear from you!

17
BONUS MATERIAL (DOMAINS)

This is just a little bit of supplementary material on some special cases involving domains. It was too long to include in the domains chapter, and I wanted to keep that moving, but I thought you might find it useful so I stuck it back here. Too much information is never a bad thing, right?

Brand/Business/Name Domain

First off, all of the best practices I just covered for the keyword-rich domain also work for the brand/business/name domain. You want to make sure you get a .com, .net, or .org version of the domain, at a reasonable market rate of $10-$15. If your business name (or your personal name) is already taken, I would recommend adding a modifier to it rather than going with a weird extension because you know how I feel about those.

. . .

Example: if LoriCulwell.com had been taken (when I set that site up a million years ago), I would have gone with something like LoriCulwell.net, LoriCulwell.org, or even LoriCulwellAuthor.com. I would not have gone with something like LoriCulwell.author or LoriCulwell.online, because I just do not think people can type those last two in, plus Google doesn't like them.

Once you find something you can live with, you might also want to extend the registration for a longer period of time (like, up to ten years), and you might want to put it on auto-renew so there's no risk of losing it. After all, you're probably going to always want to own the website for your own name.

My final word on this goes without saying, but I'm going to say it anyway: It's always a good idea to run a trademark check to see if someone else has already trademarked that name. You can do that for free over at: https://www.uspto.gov/trademarks/search

Transferring Your Domain

If you already have a domain at another registrar, you can actually transfer that domain anywhere you want. So if you just learned that you can get a domain at NameCheap for $10 - $15, you can transfer your domain over there and start paying that!

That's correct, people. If your domain registrar is charging you $50/year to renew your domain, you can take your domain to a lower-priced registrar and start paying a lower price for annual renewal right now. Really!

. . .

Another reason you might want to transfer a domain is if a designer or developer originally registered your domain for you. As I mentioned before, you want all of your stuff in your own name, so you'll want to reach out to them ASAP and tell them you want to transfer the domain over to yourself.

They will know *exactly* what you mean. They will probably try to talk you out of leaving, but stay strong! You now know that you don't have to keep overpaying!

The top two most popular places to register a domain are NameCheap and GoDaddy (though there are many, many more!), and each has a very clear process for transferring your domain to their company—and if you get stuck, each of them will be more than happy to help you, so don't be afraid to call tech support. You'll need to "unlock" the domain on the side of the current registrar, which might cause a little drama, but think about all that money you'll be saving!

You'll start this process by typing your domain name into the white "find a domain" box at the registrar where you want to transfer the domain (probably NameCheap if you're taking my advice). The receiving registrar will then tell you that you'll need to go over and "unlock" your domain at its current registrar.

The easiest way to do this is to call your current registrar, tell them you're breaking up with them and moving to another registrar, and have them walk you through unlocking the domain and generating the necessary code.

You'd think this would be awkward, and it might very well be (especially if they start trying to convince you not to leave), but, again, think of all that money you'll save, especially if you're keeping that domain for the long term! Also, remember— you're mad at them for overcharging you.

Once you get the unlock code, go back to the receiving registrar, finish the process, and pay.

Domain transfers actually take around five-to-seven days to actually complete on the registrar's side. You should get several emails from both registrars letting you know how the process is going.

You'll probably also get a couple of emails from the outgoing registrar (and maybe even a phonecall!), giving you a chance to change your mind (which you will not). These are all just informational emails and calls, so you don't need to do anything with them (though I would keep all of them until you get the final email from the *new* registrar).

Yes, that was a lengthy explanation, but I didn't want you to feel left out if you registered your domain somewhere else.

Premium Domains

. . .

As I've made pretty clear, I advise people not to buy premium domains, and especially not when setting up a brand-new business. What I do advise is this: Buy whatever $10 version of the domain you can find, launch the idea, and then let it earn that premium domain. Save every penny of revenue that domain makes, and then the minute you earn what the premium domain costs, buy it. That's what I call a green light from the universe! But since I know some of you are going to ignore me and shell out the big bucks for the domain anyway, here are some negotiation tips for you.

Remember our sourdough bread story? Here's how I would approach acquiring sourdough.onet. That domain is, in fact, for sale, and here we see that someone wants $8,999 for it.

First, never pay sticker price for a premium domain right off the bat. If your life is going to be incomplete if you don't own sourdough.org, to the point where you are willing to break off four figures for it, please just take a deep breath and enter into some negotiations first. Once a domain's price leaves the realm of a "regular price," it goes from being a thing you can impulse buy to being a piece of property, and you should proceed accordingly.

Sadly, there is no such thing as an "official" domain appraisal, but you should go over to https://www.godaddy.com/domain-value-appraisal and enter in the domain name, just to double check that the asking price is in the ballpark (and to get some proof to back up what you're going to do next).

What I would do in this case is reach out to the registrar/ broker that is holding the domain (via their "Contact Us" form, NOT through the "Buy Now" interface they want you to use). Start a conversation about this domain where you offer half of whatever they say the sticker price is.

When the registrar gets back to you with a counter offer, stay cool. Do *not* say anything that indicates to them that you want this domain. Don't say, "My grandfather owned a sourdough bakery." Don't say, "I just got $4 million in venture capital and sourdough.org is in my business plan." Don't say ANYTHING that would cause them to think you want to buy this domain more than they want to sell it. Just say a number, then wait for them to say a number.

Again, think of this like a real estate transaction or like buying a car. I have negotiated the purchase of some crazy-expensive domains on behalf of clients and have rarely paid asking price for one, so I know this tactic works.

Once you settle on a price, you will either be asked to pay with a credit card, or you will enter into an online "escrow" process. I'm sure this goes without saying, but I'm about to go all caps to make a point. DO NOT PAY CASH. DO NOT WIRE TRANSFER. DO NOT PAY WITH A CHECK. DO NOT PAY WITH A DEBIT CARD.

My point here is this: do not transfer cash money of any kind to pay for a domain (or really, to pay for anything this expensive). You need the protection provided by a credit card company, should the registrar not transfer the domain over to you (and remember from the last section, it takes five to seven days for a domain transfer to settle). You want to be able to call up your credit card company if something goes wrong and say, "I did not receive this domain, so please reverse this charge."

Also, if you pay with a credit card, you get the cash back (if your card offers that), which can be a nice little bonus.

· · ·

If the domain is owned by a private party and you are buying it directly from them, that's even more reason to use an official third party like https://www.escrow.com/. You do not want to be transferring thousands of dollars over to a random person and then waiting for that domain to settle. That is going to be a very bad week for you even if you do get that domain. Consider your blood pressure!

The bottom line is this: if you have your heart set on a premium domain, negotiate first and pay with a credit card.

Break the Domain Hoarding-Habit by Using the One-Year Rule

This is a rule I have implemented for myself over the years, and it is helping me whittle down my extensive collection of undeveloped domains.

If you're the kind of person (like me) who has what they think is a great idea and then immediately goes over and searches to see if the domain is available, this section is not only going to be relevant to you, but it is going to end up saving you a lot of money.

Because here's the thing: creative people have a ton of ideas, and not all of them are winners. If you are in the habit of impulse buying idea-based domains, you probably have at least 100 domains that are just sitting there gathering dust.

. . .

I'm sorry if that last statement was triggering. I've had to deal with this problem myself, so I know it hurts.

Don't get me wrong—I'm not throwing shade at serial domain buyers. I do, however, think that you should have a rule for yourself so you don't end up consistently wasting money on domains that don't get used. You'll also need to admit to yourself that what you think is a great domain is not worth anything unless you develop it.

Hopefully after you go through this entire guide, you will love setting up websites so much, you will actually start going through your domain collection and executing on some of these ideas. But if not, it might be time to let some of them go.

I will challenge you to start cleaning out your domain collection over the course of the next year, because it will not only save you money, it will help you focus your energy on worthwhile projects. As you'll recall, I recommend only buying domains for a one-year period. I find that if you haven't done anything with the idea for a year, you're probably not going to.

Story time: a few years ago I thought it would be funny to make a website called "ClownaDay.com" where I posted a photo of a clown every single day.

Shockingly, I never got around to that amazing idea.

. . .

So, when NameCheap (or whatever registrar you're using) sends you the email saying it's time to renew, be honest with yourself: have you given that idea any further thought since you bought the domain?

If not, let it go! Do not renew it, and don't look back. Chances are pretty good it will still be there if you decide to go back and re-purchase it in a year or two. Holding on to a portfolio of worthless domains is just dragging you down, both financially and mentally. Admit it: You do not feel great when you log to your registrar account, only to be confronted with hundreds of domains you have bought, held on to, and not developed. Start purging these over the next year or two, and you'll find that you not only feel better, but you'll enjoy having that extra money. I would apply this rule to any domain for which you paid $10 - $20. This is a good habit to get into and will save you a lot of money in the long run.

Yes, it can hurt to admit that you didn't take any action on that idea, but this can free up money to put into your active projects! Maybe you fell out of love with the idea, maybe you were going to do a collab with someone that didn't pan out, or maybe you just ran out of time. Whatever the case, one year is long enough. If you haven't done it by the renewal date, do yourself a favor and move on.

If one of your domains would be considered "premium," you might want to contact a broker like HugeDomains or the broker you originally bought it from to see if they can sell it for you. Remember though, developed domains sell better, so consider putting a Wordpress installation on that sucker and getting it some traffic before you try to sell it.

. . .

Also, don't beat yourself up for hanging on to domains for too long. You're learning now, and that's what counts!

References/Resources
    Keyword Research software I recommend:
    http://kwfinder.com
    Trademark Check:
    https://www.uspto.gov/trademarks/search
    Reasonably priced domain name registrars
    NameCheap.com
    GoDaddy.com
    domain.com
    domains.google.com

Got More Questions?

Is there still a single other thing you wanted to know about domain names that I didn't cover? Fantastic! Please come over and tell that to me.

    Here are some places you can reach me:
    www.loriculwell.com
    twitter.com/loriculwell

18
YOU MADE IT!!

That's it! You made it! Congratulations. I hope you're feeling empowered—and that your new website is up and running!

This is the part where I would ordinarily sign off with some grand conclusion and tell you how proud I am of you (which I totally am!), but this isn't really the end, because this guide is a work in progress. I will be updating it periodically, incorporating the feedback I get along the way. So instead of saying goodbye, I'll ask you: Did you find you got stuck on one part of the process? Is there something you feel like I didn't cover? Are there things that needed more explanation? Let me know!

And, of course, if this guide has just changed your life and you would simply like to say a nice thing or leave a review, that would also be grand! I look forward to hearing from you!

WHAT ELSE CAN I TEACH YOU?

If you have enjoyed our time together so much that you would like to read some other stuff I've written, here are some other books in the "Funny You Should Ask" series!

How to Do Search Engine Optimization: SEO for Marketing, Blogging, and More

How to Self-Publish a Book: Getting Your Book Out There on Amazon and Beyond

How to Market a Book: The Hilariously Detailed Guide to Author Marketing and Book Promotion

How to Sell More Books: The Missing Piece of Your Author Marketing Strategy

How to Publish Low Content Books: Publishing Journals, Notebooks, and More on KDP

www.ingramcontent.com/pod-product-compliance
Lightning Source LLC
LaVergne TN
LVHW010323070526
838199LV00065B/5646